Kasia Lipska

JAKE HALPERN is a frequent contributor to *The New Yorker* and *The New York Times Magazine*, the author of *Fame Junkies* and *Braving Home*, and the coauthor of four young adult novels. He is a fellow of Morse College at Yale University. His hour-long radio story "Switched at Birth" is one of the NPR program *This American Life*'s seven most popular shows ever.

Additional Praise for *Bad Paper*

"An enjoyable and educational read, with stories that sound too good to be true and word-for-word conversations that a Hollywood screenwriter couldn't make up."
—Jonathan Epstein, *The Buffalo News*

"Terrific . . . Completely fascinating."   —*Bloomberg View*

"With a nod to Elmore Leonard, *Bad Paper* seeks a bit of love for certain bad or not-so-nice people. . . . [Halpern] is an excellent writer."   —*Bookforum*

"I read Jake Halpern's book *Bad Paper* as if it were a thriller, staying up late to see what happened to these people buying and selling debt on the down low."   —Lisa J. Servon, *Public Books*

"A dramatic rise-and-fall tale . . . Halpern brings unexpected literary heft to the world of debt collection."   —*Kirkus Reviews*

"By fostering a greater understanding of the workings of debt collection, [*Bad Paper*] sheds enough light into the shadows to compel readers to push for change."   —*Publishers Weekly*

"*Bad Paper* is nonfiction that reads like the finest thriller: suspenseful and frightening, eye-opening, and even, at times, funny. Jake Halpern's fascinating, fearless tour of the underworld of debt collections introduces us to a cast of characters—the (mostly) men behind the scary phone calls—who deserve to be the stars of the next great HBO drama."
—Joseph Finder, bestselling author of
Suspicion and *Paranoia*

"*Bad Paper* is a riveting tale, fast-paced and filled with unforgettable characters. It is also a deeply reported and powerful exploration of America's shadow economy."

—David Grann, author of *The Lost City of Z*

"Jake Halpern knows how to follow the money. Only a consummate reporter could have achieved such an intimate view of the two debt collectors he chronicles here. And because he really knows how to tell a story, we can't take our eyes off this nasty business."

—Anne Fadiman, National Book Critics Circle Award–winning author of *The Spirit Catches You and You Fall Down*

"*Bad Paper* is a terrific achievement—for the wonderful Ponzi-scheme absurdity of the story, for the outsized characters and the skeptical sympathy they elicit. It's a book that hangs out in that gray and widening zone where the civilization we take for granted starts to break down, and it reads like Michael Lewis with a sense of the abyss. It's about downward mobility and the subtle apocalypse and it feels important—important in the way few books ever are."

—Gideon Lewis-Kraus, author of *A Sense of Direction*

"Jake Halpern's gripping tale provides an unprecedented view into the criminal underbelly of consumer finance. It's required reading not only for everybody with creditors on the line, but for anybody who cares about money or debt."

—Felix Salmon, senior editor, *Fusion*

BAD PAPER

INSIDE

THE

SECRET WORLD

OF

DEBT COLLECTORS

JAKE HALPERN

PICADOR   FARRAR, STRAUS AND GIROUX   NEW YORK

www.picadorusa.com
www.twitter.com/picadorusa • www.facebook.com/picadorusa
picadorbookroom.tumblr.com

Picador® is a U.S. registered trademark and is used by Farrar, Straus and Giroux
under license from Pan Books Limited.

For book club information, please visit www.facebook.com/picadorbookclub
or e-mail marketing@picadorusa.com.

Designed by Abby Kagan

The Library of Congress has cataloged the Farrar, Straus and Giroux edition as follows:

Halpern, Jake.
    Bad paper : chasing debt from Wall Street to the underworld / Jake
Halpern. — 1st Edition.
        p. cm.
    ISBN 978-0-374-10823-6 (hardcover)
    ISBN 978-0-374-71124-5 (e-book)
    1. Finance, Personal.   2. Consumer credit.   3. Collecting of accounts.
    4. Collection agencies.   I. Title.
    HG179 .H247 2014
    332.70973—dc23

                                                                    2014013576

Picador Paperback ISBN 978-1-250-07633-5

Our books may be purchased in bulk for promotional, educational, or
business use. Please contact your local bookseller or the Macmillan Corporate and
Premium Sales Department at (800) 221-7945, extension 5442, or by
e-mail at MacmillanSpecialMarkets@macmillan.com.

First published by Farrar, Straus and Giroux

First Picador Edition: October 2015

10 9 8 7 6 5 4 3 2 1

To Stephen Halpern—consummate father and friend

Be kind, for everyone you meet is engaged in a great struggle.

—AUTHOR UNKNOWN

CONTENTS

BAD PAPER

INTRODUCTION

One evening in October 2009, a former banking executive named Aaron Siegel waited impatiently in the master bedroom of a house in the Allentown neighborhood of Buffalo, New York. As he stared at the room's old fireplace and then out the window to the sleepy street beyond, he tried *not* to think about his investors and the $14 million that they had entrusted to him. Aaron was no stranger to money. He had grown up in one of the city's wealthiest and most famous families. His father, Herb Siegel, was a legendary playboy and the founder of a hugely profitable personal-injury law firm. During his late teenage years, Aaron had essentially lived unchaperoned in a sprawling, hundred-year-old mansion. His sister, Shana, recalls the parties that she hosted—lavish affairs with plenty of champagne—and how their private school classmates would often spend the night, as if the place were a clubhouse for the young and privileged.

On this particular day in October, Aaron wondered how exactly he had gotten into his current predicament. His career had started with such promise. He had earned his M.B.A. from the highly regarded Simon Graduate School of Business at the University of Rochester. He had taken a job at HSBC and completed the bank's executive training course in London. By all indications, he was well on his way to a very respectable career in the financial world. Aaron was smart, hardworking, and ambitious. All he had to do was keep moving up the corporate ladder; instead, he had decided to take a gamble.

In the summer of 2008, Aaron launched his own private equity fund in an elegant old home at 448 Franklin Street in Buffalo. He claimed the master bedroom for his office. His company, which he dubbed Franklin Asset Management, focused on distressed consumer debt; basically, he was interested in buying up the right to collect unpaid credit-card bills. There is a vast market for unpaid consumer debts—not just credit-card debts but auto loans, medical loans, gym fees, payday loans, overdue cell phone tabs, old utility bills, even delinquent book club accounts. Indeed, American consumers owe a grand total of $11.28 trillion, of which roughly $831 billion is delinquent or unpaid. Some 30 million consumers are currently being hounded over at least one loan; and each of these debtors owes, on average, $1,458.

Many consumers assume that when they receive a call about an unpaid debt—from Bank of America, or Verizon, or Aaron's Furniture Rental—they are actually speaking with an official from that company. Not so. The original creditor has often written off that debt as a loss years before and sold it at a fraction of its value to speculators who hope to collect on it and turn a tidy profit. Much has been said and written about the subprime mortgage crisis and how risky loans were issued, bundled, spliced, diced, and sold. Far less has been written about the enormous quantity of consumer debt that is bought, bundled, and sold each year; those who trade in such debt call it "paper" and they typically buy it and sell it for pennies on the dollar.

That was Aaron's business. If he could buy debts with "face values" of $1,500 for $15—and if his agencies could collect just 10 percent of what was owed—he could make a fortune. What he needed was capital, so he used his connections from his school days, and from the banking world, to court eight investors. In the ensuing year and a half, he would use their money to buy $1.5 billion worth of bad debts. This would be his trial run. If all went smoothly, he would soon launch another fund, with even more money in it.

But all did not go smoothly.

Some of the deals that Aaron made were hugely profitable, while others proved more troublesome. As he soon discovered, after creditors sell off unpaid debts, those debts enter a financial netherworld where strange things can happen. A gamut of players including publicly traded companies, hedge fund operators, professional debt collectors, street hustlers, ex-cons, and lawyers all work together, and against one another, to recoup every penny on every dollar. In this often-lawless marketplace, large portfolios of debt—usually in the form of spreadsheets holding debtor names, contact information, and balances—are bought, sold, and sometimes simply stolen.

Stolen.

This was the word that was foremost in Aaron's mind on that October afternoon in 2009. He had strong reason to believe that a portfolio of paper—his paper—had been stolen and was now being worked by one of the many small collection agencies on the impoverished and crime-ridden East Side of Buffalo. Using his spreadsheets, this agency was now calling his debtors and collecting on debt that was rightfully his. This was *not* a problem that Aaron was used to handling. There had been no classes at the Simon Graduate School of Business on how to apprehend thieves who had appropriated your assets. He could, of course, call the police or the state attorney general; but, by the time that they intervened, the paper would be wrung dry, worthless. His problem was more fundamental, more pressing. At this point, he didn't know exactly how many files had been stolen, but he knew that he needed immediate intervention.

Fortunately, Aaron had someone to call.

His name was Brandon Wilson. A former armed robber, Brandon had spent roughly ten years in prison, and now liked to boast that he made far more in debt collections than he ever did robbing banks. Brandon worked as Aaron's most valued "debt broker," buying and selling portfolios on Aaron's behalf. He also served as his emissary to the collections industry's many unsavory precincts. And at this very moment—as Aaron waited impatiently in the old, wood-paneled master bedroom at 448 Franklin Street—Brandon was en route to Buffalo with a car full of his associates, mainly ex-cons, some of them armed and all of them determined to help fix the problem. Their goal was simple: rescue the stolen accounts.

The following pages tell the story of Aaron and Brandon's unlikely partnership and track the stolen portfolio of debt they set out to retrieve. To its handlers, that portfolio was just a spreadsheet containing the names and social security numbers of debtors and the amounts they owed; but that same spreadsheet was also a collection of stories about Americans whose financial lives had unraveled. This book chronicles some of those lives and simultaneously explores a thriving industry that buys and sells old loans like precious jewels. In many blighted neighborhoods, in Buffalo and elsewhere, small shops that collect debt—often by unsavory means—are sources of employment and engines of mobility for people who, otherwise, would be hard-pressed to find work. Across the country, a much larger industry traffics in old debts, frequently using dubious methods to pressure debtors into paying up, even on debts they have already settled or for which they are no longer liable.

Ever since 2006, the Federal Trade Commission (FTC) has ranked "debt collection" as its second-biggest source of complaints from consumers, following only "identity theft." It has not done much, however, to clean things up. In 2009, it brought just one "enforcement action" against a company for collections violations; since then, it has done little more. Banks, creditors, and regulators are at last starting to crack down on certain conspicuous abuses but the system as a whole remains dysfunctional and largely unsupervised. The newly created Consumer Financial Protection Bureau focuses on policing 175 of the nation's largest collectors, while thousands of smaller companies escape its scrutiny. Debt collection remains, in many regards, a shadowy corner of the economy—where financial misfortune is bought, sold, and exploited. As sensational as this may sound, it is exactly what one might expect in a country that is driven by profit, mired in debt, and not fully able or willing to tame the marketplace that is created when these two forces meet.

PART ONE

STOLEN NUMBERS

1

THE $14 MILLION GAMBLE

In 2005, when he was thirty-one years old, Aaron Siegel decided to leave his job on Wall Street and move back to his hometown. He was drawn to Buffalo—the self-proclaimed "city of no illusions"—because of its modest scale, its historic neighborhoods, and its general lack of pretension. After so much time in Manhattan and London, something about Buffalo was refreshingly real. What's more, the Siegel family name meant something there and it lent Aaron not just credibility or prestige, but a sense that he belonged—that he mattered. Aaron returned to Buffalo, along with his wife, who was also from upstate New York, and he took a job at a local division of Bank of America specializing in private wealth management. He resolved to stay there until he could figure something else out. The only problem was that he had almost no work to do. "I spent my days spinning around in a chair and throwing pencils at the ceiling," Aaron said. "There was nothing to do. There's very little private wealth to manage here."

There weren't a great many banking opportunities in Buffalo;

in truth, there weren't all that many professional opportunities at all. At least one industry, however, was booming: debt collection. Buffalo is a major hub for debt collection and is sometimes even called the industry's capital. This is in large part because one of the biggest collection agencies in the nation, known as Great Lakes Collection Bureau, was once based there. GE Capital purchased Great Lakes in 1997, and soon afterward, many of the company's managers were laid off and opted to strike out on their own. Their companies thrived and expanded. In the greater Buffalo area, more than five thousand people now earn a living as debt collectors. That's more than the number of taxi drivers, bakers, butchers, steelworkers, roofers, crane operators, hotel clerks, and brick masons combined.

As a former banker, Aaron was intrigued that so many people in his midst were toiling to collect on debts that his employer—the bank—had given up on and sold to debt buyers at huge discounts. He sensed an opportunity and, in the fall of 2005, he started his own collection agency. He used $125,000 from his personal savings, bought some "paper," and threw himself—rather blindly—into the world of collections. His plan was to continue working at Bank of America by day and run the collection agency after hours.

When it came to hiring collectors, Buffalo proved to be an auspicious locale, both because there were so many veteran collectors to hire and because so many of the city's other residents were so eager to find paying work. Buffalo remains among the poorest cities in the nation. Almost one-third of the people within its limits live in poverty—double the national average. Growing up in a very affluent family, Aaron says that he rarely interacted with the city's poorer residents. "I knew they existed," he told me. "These were folks that you bumped into going to the store, but there wasn't a whole lot of interaction because Buffalo is very stratified." Yet when Aaron launched his own collection agency, these were precisely the sorts of people who applied for work—and their ranks included ex-cons, drug addicts, twenty-somethings without high school diplomas, and a variety of other hard-luck cases.

"Oh my God, they were like thugs," recalled Aaron. "Everybody had their hustle and flow or whatever the hell it was—why they were the best, the greatest." He quickly came to realize, however, that the more clean-cut types simply wouldn't get the job done. As he put it: "You realize that you're sitting on an investment and you've hired a bunch of boy scouts who can't turn any money." What he needed were telephone hustlers. The problem with the hustlers, explained Aaron, was that they hustled not just the debtors, but him as well. One of the first truly great collectors that Aaron hired—an overweight, womanizing, aspiring bodybuilder—robbed him of several thousand dollars by counterfeiting the firm's checks.

Eventually, Aaron hired a floor manager—a young, handsome guy in his mid-twenties, who asked to be identified by his middle name, Rob. Rob understood collectors. He took it as a given, for example, that many of his collectors either used or sold drugs. In one of his stints as a manager, Rob bought his team "three cases of whippets"—steel cartridges filled with nitrous oxide—for hitting their goal. "You have to have a little hustle in you to collect," he explained. "Certainly, if you are selling bags of pot to college kids, you have that natural ability." One day, Rob had to help break up a fight that began when a collector overcharged his co-worker for a bag of cocaine. Their punishment, recalls Rob, was simply being sent home for the day. Above all, says Rob, the collectors needed "someone they could relate to"—someone who could be a "bridge" to Aaron. "I was that bridge."

Rob's biggest challenge was making sure that one of the agency's best collectors made it to work each day. On many occasions, Rob confiscated his car keys and insisted that he spend the night with Rob at his house. "He was a very intelligent guy, but he was also your average stoner who didn't think of the day ahead until that morning," recalled Rob. "He was extremely lazy and smoked a massive amount of pot. At the time, he was twenty-three and he didn't understand the whole concept of work responsibility." When he did show up, however, he was masterful at the "talk-off"—the spiel given to debtors in order to encourage, shame, and intimidate them into paying. This particular collector was a "killer" and a "beast" on the phone, Rob said.

To this day, Rob recalls his talk-off with great admiration: "He would ask a question, which he knew the answer to, but when he got the debtor's response, he flipped it on them. For example, maybe the debtor bought a dishwasher for a thousand dollars from Sears. The debtor would say, 'I didn't have a job at the time.' Then he would say, 'But I have paperwork right here saying that you worked at Rich Stadium at the time, and now I would like a statement from you because I am going to have to explain to the banks that you were lying.' He'd get them into a trap. He'd get them to lie, then he'd call them on it, and then—in five minutes—they were writing a check." According to Aaron, his star employee collected as much as $20,000 a month.

Aaron took it as a given that some of his collectors, the good and bad alike, might quit at a moment's notice. The industry was famous for employing "hoppers," who simply stopped coming to work one day and "hopped" to another agency where they thought they might do better for themselves. One of the most famous hoppers in Buffalo was a man of exceedingly short stature known as "Matt the Midget." "He had these extended pedals on his car so his feet could reach," Aaron said. When he showed up for an interview at Aaron's agency, Matt the Midget delighted Aaron's employees by leaping into the air and tapping his forehead with his own feet. Aaron's agency offered him a job, but unfortunately, Matt the Midget never showed up for work. Not even once.

What made it all worth it for Aaron was that he was making money. When he purchased an especially good portfolio of debt, the profits were astronomical. For example, he obtained one portfolio for $28,526, collected more than $90,000 on it in just six weeks, and then sold the remaining, uncollected accounts for $31,000. On that portfolio, he made a whopping net return of 199 percent. Aaron bought another portfolio of debt for $33,387, collected more than $147,000 on it in four months, and then sold the remaining accounts for $33,123. On this portfolio, his net return was 264 percent. Of course, not all of his deals proved to be this wildly profitable; but, on the whole, he was doing well with almost all of the paper that he purchased. This was in no small part because in 2006 he had begun buying paper from a debt broker named Brandon Wilson. Initially, at least, Aaron knew very little about Brandon. A business associate had recommended him, and right away, Brandon began to prove his worth—supplying good paper, with "plenty of meat on the bone" as they say in the business. "The paper that I bought from him performed wonderfully," recalled Aaron.

During the day, while he toiled away at Bank of America, Aaron began spending more time with one of his co-workers: a beautiful young brunette named Andrea. Andrea grew up in an Italian-American family in the nearby town of Batavia, worked for a few years as a teacher, and then took a job with Bank of America at its corporate headquarters in Charlotte, North Carolina. She returned home to western New York and arrived at the Bank of America offices in Buffalo with a sense of deflation that mirrored Aaron's. "There were like nine people in our office and they were all like six days from dying," she told me.

Then she saw Aaron.

"I was standing at the receptionist desk, and he walks by, and I remember in my mind remarking, 'He's got a nice suit on. Okay, maybe this isn't so bad.'" On one of their next encounters, Andrea was stranded in the parking lot with a flat tire, and Aaron came to her rescue. The only problem was that he didn't know how to change a tire properly and he ended up damaging her car. Somehow he managed to make light of the debacle, and his own ineptitude, which Andrea found strangely endearing. They were soon spending more time together and, eventually, started having an affair. "I don't think I was emotionally ready to be married in the first place, but—up until then—I was doing a very good job of faking it," Aaron told me. "Really, it was just terrible judgment."

To this day, Andrea isn't sure what Aaron was thinking at the time. "I don't really know what the draw was—not wanting to be with his wonderful blond wife that everyone loved in order to date a crazy Italian. Who does that? Nobody." Aaron ultimately decided to leave his wife and, on top of that, his job at Bank of America as well. "He basically put his life in a jar and shook the shit out of it," said Andrea. Looking back, Aaron's father, Herb, says that Andrea—whom he calls a "femme fatale"—was a very bad influence on his son. "She's very attractive and very seductive," he warned me.

Aaron's younger sister, Shana, puzzled over her brother's

transformation from Wall Street banker to owner and opera-
tor of a small collection agency in Buffalo. She would stop by
his agency and wonder what her brother had gotten himself
into. "I'd be in his office, seeing the people that were coming
in, and I was like: *What the hell? What do you got going on
here?* It felt shady." She viewed all of it as being a far cry from
the high hopes that her family had for Aaron. Shana recalls
that Aaron had nice artwork on the walls of his personal office
but that elsewhere in the agency the carpet was ratty, the rail-
ings were rickety, and the employees seemed sketchy. "It was
like he was trying to put gold rims on a dilapidated car," she
said. "It was like he was trying to make my father's office out
of something that was not as nice."

Aaron's father, Herb Siegel, was a legend in Buffalo. He was
a successful divorce lawyer and the founder of Siegel, Kelleher
& Kahn—a hugely profitable law firm that handled divorces
and personal-injury cases. In the early 1990s, *The Buffalo News*
ran a lengthy profile on Herb, describing his "Gatsby-esque
parties" and his lavish lifestyle. The article depicted Herb at
work in his "two spectacularly renovated Victorian mansions"
under the soft glow of chandeliers. "He enjoys the perks that
come from sitting atop his law firm: The respectful associates
whose offices were once the sitting rooms and servants' bedrooms of the 19th century mansion . . . Clients can't help no-
ticing the glamour, the elegance . . . [especially] the women
who come to him at the most difficult time of their lives and
tearfully whisper revealing details about their most personal
encounters in their marriages. He is someone who can solve
their problems. He has the power to make it better. They
adore him."

Herb's own marriages were tumultuous. He married and
divorced three times, though not all of his separations were

bitter. His second wife, for example, subsequently took a job as his bookkeeper. His third wife, Aaron's mother—Joyce Siegel—actually started off as a client. When she first met Herb, she was in the midst of a divorce, and Herb's office was representing her. Initially, Joyce was working with another lawyer at the firm, but when she broke down in tears, the lawyer summoned Herb for help. This was Herb's specialty—he knew how to handle even the most distraught of clients. He walked in, told her to stop crying, and took over her case. "Herb usurped the client in more ways than one," Joyce recalled.

Joyce says that she was initially drawn to Herb because he had the aura of a "man about town." "You know how women are. They like power and money, and, in the situation I was in, I didn't have any of that." They eventually married, but Joyce says it was rocky from the start because Herb would stay out late, leaving her at home, worrying—and then simmering. "I reached a point where I wouldn't even leave the porch light on for him. I was really hoping, secretly, that he'd fall and break his neck or crash on the way home. Then he would come home, he'd [usually] been drinking—I'm sure he'd been with women—and he would go into the bedroom to wake up Aaron." At the time, Aaron was an infant and Joyce says she would plead with her husband, unsuccessfully, to let Aaron sleep. "I'd hear Ari"—her nickname for Aaron—"in there, tossing and turning, trying to get back to sleep. He was such a good little boy. He wasn't a crier."

As his law firm continued to prosper, Herb began looking for a new, grander home for his family within the city's historic district around the Albright-Knox Art Gallery. One day, he and Joyce went to see a gorgeous old mansion on Soldiers Place, one of the city's most prestigious addresses. The house, situated kitty-corner from a mansion designed by Frank Lloyd

Wright, was a stately edifice built in 1905. It boasted seven bedrooms, five bathrooms, and more than five thousand square feet of floor space. During their initial tour of the house, Joyce was unconvinced: "I remember being up in the room on the third floor, in what was like a pool room, and I was thinking, 'God, I don't know, this is so big.'" Then, without consulting his wife, Herb said to the agent, "We'll take it."

Aaron speculates that his father purchased the mansion with the intention of flipping it whenever the opportunity arose. "I think he probably put it on the market as soon as he bought it," says Aaron. "No sentimental attachments there—that's how he is." When Herb finally did sell the house, more than two decades later, the buyer was the Canadian government, which wanted a suitable home for the head of its consulate. Herb sold the house for an enormous profit. When he inked the deal with the Canadians, Herb was amused to see that the contract bore the seal of the British Crown. "He ripped off the Queen of England," said Aaron. "That doesn't happen every day."

As the years passed, Joyce became increasingly unhappy with her marriage and the family dynamics at Soldiers Place. She eventually ended the marriage and moved out of Soldiers Place, leaving Aaron and Shana—who wanted to stay in their childhood home—behind. The house was never the same after that. What ensued was the much-idealized scenario that many an American teenager has dreamed of: a mansion stocked with food and liquor, a permissive father, and an open-door policy for friends and classmates. Shana recalls this time in her life with great nostalgia: "I would say to my dad, 'I'm having thirty couples here before the date dance, and I expect you not to come home for the whole night.' And he'd be like, 'Okay.'" It was a dream come true for Shana: "We're fifteen years old and we're all sitting around drinking champagne in this grand house."

As permissive as Herb could be, he was—in other, important ways—quite overbearing. According to Shana, Herb "had grandiose ideas of what my brother would be" and this weighed on Aaron "terribly." Aaron understood his father's expectations implicitly. In Herb's view, says Aaron, people were either "losers" or "very successful"—and it was always based on how much money they made. Herb's hopes may have weighed heavily on his son, but Herb shrugged this off as inevitable. As Herb told me, "Look, when you come from a family like ours, you're always going to be striving. You're going to want to do something better than your father. I think that goes with the territory."

For Aaron, the collections industry offered both financial reward and voyeuristic access to the city's seedier side. According to Rob, Aaron's floor manager at the agency, his boss was both fascinated and repulsed by the business: "Where Aaron came from, with a private high school and prestigious family, that was a different world. He liked this scene, in a way. You know how opposites attract? You know, you have the good girl dating the bad biker dude—she is intrigued. Maybe he was like that." Even so, Rob added, "when he had a chance not to get his hands dirty anymore, he took that route."

Aaron's chance, it turns out, came with the realization that he didn't have to operate a collection agency himself. Instead, he could buy portfolios of debt and then place them at other agencies, which would collect on the debt for him. These agencies would operate on a "contingency basis," keeping a percentage of whatever they collected. From Rob's perspective, Aaron's decision made sense. "When he saw the potential in debt buying—where he could avoid lawsuits, avoid dealing with collectors and the bullshit that comes with that—he thought, *I can make just as much buying and selling.* It has to do with his personality. Instead of cleaning his house, he would rather hire a maid."

Aaron's plan appeared to be a smart one. His connections and experience as a banker in Manhattan—combined with his real-life experiences in the trenches of Buffalo—would make him uniquely qualified for this new venture. In the language of the collections industry, Aaron would operate as a "privately financed debt buyer." A 2010 report by the Legal Aid Society and several other nonprofits speculates that there are roughly five hundred such buyers in the United States and concludes that little is known about how they operate. This often works out well for the buyers. After all, it is much easier to operate with minimal public scrutiny. An investment banker at one of the big Wall Street houses told me that he could never invest in "distressed consumer debt" because ever since his firm's government bailout, its unofficial motto has been, "We cannot fuck the American taxpayer." He had to run all of his deals by the PR department; thus, even if he could make a killing on an investment involving consumer debt, the PR people would likely say no.

There have been privately financed debt buyers operating in the United States since well before the Civil War. At that time, there was no uniform paper currency and if you wanted to buy a piece of property, say—and didn't have the money—you could simply write a promissory note. In fact, this is precisely what Abraham Lincoln did in 1833 when he acquired a general store from a man named Reuben Radford. In financing this purchase, he signed a promissory note to Radford for $379.82. The business fared poorly and when Lincoln proved unable to repay what he had borrowed, Radford sold his promissory note—which was merely a piece of "paper"—to the debt buyer Peter

Van Bergen. Van Bergen then successfully sued Lincoln, ultimately prompting a sheriff to seize and auction off Lincoln's surveying tools, saddle, and bridle. Years later, Lincoln effectively switched sides and spent much of his legal career suing debtors on behalf of clients large and small. He also worked on the side for the equivalent of a credit bureau, providing information on the financial soundness of merchants and others in the community. As James Cornelius, the curator of the Lincoln Presidential Library and Museum, put it: "He ratted out his friends."

The marketplace for consumer debt, as we know it today, traces its origins to the late 1980s and early 1990s. One of the early pioneers of the debt-buying industry was a flamboyant self-made billionaire named Bill Bartmann, whose ability to promote his businesses—and himself—rivals that of Donald Trump and Don King. He grew up in Dubuque, Iowa, but dropped out of high school and left his home at the age of fourteen—at which point he claims to have taken up residence in the hayloft of a barn and joined a gang of ruffians known as the "Manor Boys." "The farmer who owned the barn found out I was living up there and then burned the few clothes that I had left," Bartmann told me. Bartmann eventually went into business, and grew rich by launching a successful oil equipment company. When oil prices crashed, in the mid-1980s, his company failed and Bartmann ended up $1 million in debt. Debt collectors started calling him around the clock.

Then, one day, his fortune changed when he saw an interesting advertisement in the newspaper. The federal government was auctioning off unpaid debts that belonged to two failed banks in Tulsa, Oklahoma. The government had bailed out the banks and taken their assets—including the unpaid debts—and was now trying to recoup its losses. This practice became more common in the early 1990s when the federal government's Resolution Trust Corporation bailed out a number of the failed financial institutions known as savings and loan associations, or S&Ls. Many of the S&Ls had made very risky loans, which ultimately caused them to fail. The government seized their assets and auctioned off nearly $500 billion of their unpaid loans. These auctions helped establish how vast quantities of unpaid debts could be priced at a discount and then sold to enterprising buyers.

At the auction in Tulsa, Bartmann ended up bidding on and winning a portfolio of unpaid debts for $13,000. To pay for it, he borrowed the $13,000 from the very same bank that was still trying to collect $1 million from him. The portfolio was a mix of various consumer loans, including auto loans, recreational vehicle loans, and home improvement loans. He promptly collected $64,000 on this portfolio. Bartmann continued buying paper from the federal government at a discount and then collecting on it with great success; within two years, he had paid off the $1 million that he owed the bank. In the early 1990s, Bartmann bought credit-card debt for the first time and entirely by accident. The credit-card accounts were simply mixed in with the other consumer loans in a portfolio he bought from the government. "Our first reaction was, *Oh crap!*" says Bartmann. "We didn't want them." The conventional wisdom at the time, says Bartmann, was that consumers were unlikely to repay old credit-card debts because they felt no sense of personal connection to the creditor. It wasn't like an auto loan where, presumably, the consumer made a single purchase and could likely remember the car, the dealer, and the dealership. This conventional wisdom proved false. These loans were very profitable to collect on—twice as profitable as his other paper—and Bartmann was soon in search of more of them.

In 1994, Bartmann recalls going directly to NationsBank, soon to be Bank of America, and offering to buy their old, unpaid credit-card accounts. When a debtor stops paying his or her credit-card bill, the banks count the balance as an asset for 180 days, during which time the bank's collectors try their very best to collect on what is owed. After that time, the Generally Accepted Accounting Principles (GAAP)—which banks must follow by law—require that these accounts no longer be counted as assets, because the money might not be collectible. Banks then "charge off" the accounts, taking a loss. Bartmann was, in effect, offering banks cash for what—on paper at least—appeared worthless or close to worthless. As he recalled: "They sold us their ugliest of the ugly for two cents on the dollar—these were four-year-old charged-off credit-card loans that had been sitting smoldering in the basement for God knows how many years—and we took them home and had an extremely good result with them." In order to maximize his returns, he also began classifying his collectors into distinct demographic groups and paired them with debtors of the same ilk: "We didn't want anyone from the NAACP calling anyone from the KKK, because that would be a nonstarter on day one."

Before long, he was buying up bad debt on a massive scale. He began bundling this debt, selling it to investors as bonds, and then using their money to buy even more debt. Bartmann's firm, Commercial Financial Services (CFS), quickly became one of the largest debt-collection companies in the nation. Bartmann played the role of newly crowned debt czar to the hilt. It was widely reported in the press that he hired former Secret Service agents to protect him, arranged to wrestle Hulk Hogan in Las Vegas, and flew thousands of employees to retreats in the Caribbean. Bartmann once boasted to a journalist that he had so much money, "If I set it all on fire, I'd be dead before it went out." But it didn't turn out that way. According to *The New York Times*, Bartmann's troubles started when someone sent an anonymous letter to credit-rating agencies, stating that CFS was giving investors a false picture of the company's financial health. The letter alleged that CFS was discreetly selling some of its debt to a "shell company"—with ties to a major shareholder at CFS—and was then using the proceeds from these sales to inflate its apparent success in collecting. Bartmann subsequently stepped down as CEO, investors began to sue, money from lenders disappeared, and CFS filed for bankruptcy.

Some might view Bartmann's story as a cautionary tale, but plenty of others saw it as an example of the fortunes that could be earned in this previously obscure niche of the financial world. After all, Bartmann's missteps didn't necessarily mean that the industry itself was toxic. If anything, by the early 2000s, as Americans in a mostly stagnant-wage economy began taking out more and more debt on their credit cards, it seemed as if the opportunities might even be greater.

Starting in the fall of 2007, Aaron Siegel began looking for investors. At this point, the economy was still booming; in October, the stock market reached its all-time high when the Dow Jones Industrial Average peaked at 14,164. Throughout the fall, Aaron called every rich person he knew in the hopes of raising millions of dollars and launching a private equity fund, which he dubbed Vintage Two. This was to be a onetime deal with a limited lifespan. Investors would make an initial investment and then, over the course of the next four years, receive returns until all of the money the fund earned was dispersed. According to the terms of the deal, for every dollar that he spent to purchase paper for the fund, Aaron would receive a 2-percent commission to help pay for his operating expenses.

His real benefit, however, would come only after the fund broke even, at which point he was entitled to 15 percent of all profits.

When courting his investors, Aaron tried to caution them about the volatile and even unsavory nature of the investment that they were about to make: "When I pitched to investors, I told them, 'Just so you know, this is a dark sector of the finance world. This is something that people don't like to talk about.'" There was potential for great profits, Aaron assured his would-be investors, but it could be risky. "This is not where you want to be with your life savings. But if you have some speculative capital, this is a good thing to roll the dice on." To entice his investors, he showed them a spreadsheet detailing the profits that he had made from ten portfolios of debt that he'd purchased in the past—roughly half of which he'd acquired from the man who'd become his closest associate, Brandon Wilson, though he made no mention of this. The returns on these portfolios were impressive. Four of them showed net gains of more than 100 percent in seven months or less; another four portfolios showed gains of more than 20 percent in a similar time period. Even in the best of times, these numbers were remarkable.

One of Aaron's challenges was to convince his investors that he had a unique and superior approach to debt buying. Aaron noted that the industry behemoths, publicly traded companies such as Encore Capital Group and Asta Funding, tended to buy "fresh" paper directly from the banks. This paper is highly valued. In all likelihood, just a few of the banks' own collectors or subcontractors had ever tried to collect on it; and these collectors likely embraced a softer, customer-service approach to collecting. A debt buyer such as Asta Funding might buy a portfolio of "fresh" paper, collect on much of it successfully, and then sell those accounts that didn't pay. In other words, the debt buyers at the top of the food chain pay more money for better paper, but generally have an easier time collecting and making money off it. Meanwhile, the debt buyers at the bottom of the food chain pay less money for older, grungier paper that is, for the most part, harder to collect on. Those debt buyers—not surprisingly—are more likely to use hard-hitting, coercive, and even illegal tactics to get debtors to pay.

There is, however, another way to make money off older paper—namely buying paper that has been bought and sold repeatedly, but has not been collected on efficiently and thus wrung dry. This is what Aaron wanted to do. He told his investors that his goal, in significant part, was to buy "grungy" paper that had been around the block but retained its value. In short, he wanted to buy paper that was not as "beaten up" as it looked. After all, Aaron reasoned, a smart buyer could capitalize on just how difficult it was to price debt accurately. A dizzying array of variables affect a portfolio of debt's true potential—including the age of the debt, how many agencies have worked it, the size of the balances, the types of credit card involved, the regions where its debtors live, the current economic climate, and many other factors. There is no single market or venue—like the NASDAQ or the New York Stock Exchange—where this kind of debt is sold. This creates a marketplace that is inherently inefficient, which makes it hugely enticing to many investors. Warren Buffett once famously said, "I'd be a bum on the street with a tin cup if the markets were efficient."

One of Aaron's investors told me that he was won over by the possibility that Aaron had found a wonderfully inefficient little market. He liked the idea that most deals were made through intermediaries—and that there was no easy way to know what the debt was really worth. You couldn't simply check on the Internet or the business section of the newspaper. "There is the potential to buy bad paper, but there is also the potential—if you are smart or savvy enough—that you should be able to exploit this shortage of information," the investor told me.

With $14 million from his investors all lined up, Aaron was poised for success. Overnight, he had gone from being the owner of a small call center, in which he had to deal with the likes of Matt the Midget, to once again being a player in the high-powered world of finance. And this time, in contrast with his stints working at big banks, he was in control of his own destiny. Aaron's next order of business was to find a few good collection agencies to work his debt.

Aaron wanted to avoid hiring the enormous mega-agencies, with their endless rows of cubicles, stretching on forever and fading off into the dreary, monochromatic horizon. In Aaron's view, these agencies had more paper than they knew what to do with. Such places often scored each and every debtor—by running a series of credit checks—and then worked only the top-scoring accounts, leaving the rest untouched. Aaron wanted smaller, hungrier shops, where he was the sole provider of paper. "This way," explained Aaron, "they have to do well for me or they don't make payroll." Such an agency might eventually go out of business, he reasoned, because it would spend too much time on each account; but while it was up and running, it would make him money. He also wanted a shop that collected aggressively—not one that was "threatening to break legs" but a place where collectors were willing to test the limits of what was allowed under the Fair Debt Collection Practices Act of 1977. This law forbids debt collectors from engaging in abusive, deceptive, or unfair practices and it places certain restrictions on how and when they can call a debtor.

Aaron knew precisely what he was looking for, and in early 2009, he found a man who promised to provide it. Shafeeq, who asked only to be identified by his middle name, was the co-owner of a small, five-man shop. Shafeeq was an ambitious young black Muslim from the impoverished East Side of Buffalo—an imposing figure of a man, roughly six and a half feet tall, and weighing more than 300 pounds. Shafeeq looked the part of a bodyguard and, in addition to running his debt-collection agency, he ran his own security business on the side. Shafeeq's intimidating appearance, however, belied a more thoughtful and soft-spoken aspect. As a child, Shafeeq was such an avid reader that he churned through each page of the *Encyclopedia Britannica* at his parents' house, in wild anticipation of the mysteries that awaited him in the volume labeled "X."

Shafeeq spent his early teenage years at a boarding school for Muslims, run by Arabs, in the suburbs of Buffalo. He eventually earned his GED, got married at the age of twenty-four, and took a job working as a debt collector, which was a complicated choice of profession for a devout Muslim. He told me that, whenever possible, he tried to honor Islam's ban on usury by collecting only the principal that debtors owed. His faith and profession intersected in other interesting ways as well. According to Shafeeq, his branch of Islam allowed polygamy, which enabled him to take a second wife—a woman who was the administrative assistant at his small collection agency. It was a tempestuous relationship. They divorced and then remarried on multiple occasions. (Getting a divorce, he told me, was simply a matter of writing out a statement and having two witnesses sign it.) The divorces took their toll on him. "Polygamy in itself is a powerful, tough thing," he told me. "You know what I mean? And it's an emotional thing. Because women can act very jealous. You know what I'm saying?"

Shafeeq's stress managing his two wives was compounded by his business woes. By the standards of the industry, he was working very low-quality paper. At one point, it had gotten so bad that Shafeeq was collecting on Radio Shack credit-card debt, some of which dated back to 1983. Just before meeting Aaron, he had purchased two portfolios of bad paper—one for $10,000 and another for $14,000—which proved so beaten-up that they were virtually uncollectible. Whenever he prayed—unrolling his prayer mat, kneeling down, and making *dua*, a Muslim prayer in which the supplicant beseeches God for help—he asked for divine intervention with his business. As if in answer to Shafeeq's prayers, Aaron called, introduced himself, and offered to buy a one-third share in his company for $25,000. Shafeeq's shop was too small to handle a large volume of paper, but Aaron could fix that.

According to the terms of the deal, Aaron would provide all of the paper, process the credit-card payments, and do the accounting. Shafeeq's collection agency would take a 50 percent commission, a third of which would go to Aaron. In short, Aaron would be in control, while Shafeeq and his co-owner—another young black Muslim—would have the headache of running the place. Looking back, Shafeeq says: "I would probably have agreed to anything at that point."

Shafeeq filed for incorporation in April 2009 and began hiring employees rapidly until soon he had an office of thirty people. Most of these employees were white and some bristled at the prospect of working for a black man—and a Muslim at that. Shafeeq heard that a few of them occasionally referred to him as a "nigger" behind his back. And so Shafeeq eventually decided that operations would run most smoothly if he told his employees that Aaron was, essentially, the sole proprietor of the business and he was merely the supervisor. "The world is crazy and screwed up," he said. "People think in screwed-up ways and people are racist. They don't even know they're racist. People hate. They're angry. And instead of trying to change it, you know, it's better to just learn how to maneuver inside of it the best way you can."

What made it all worth it was the quality of the paper that Aaron began to deliver. In the past, Shafeeq never had the resources or the connections to buy high-quality paper, which is typically sold in bulk—either directly by creditors or by the big debt buyers. He was simply too far down the food chain. Aaron transformed that. He was soon providing credit-card debt with fairly recent charge-off dates; and, according to Shafeeq, the money started pouring in. Shafeeq began taking home $10,000 a month, which was far more than he had ever earned in the past. "It was a whole new world," he said.

Now that he was flush with cash, Shafeeq eventually decided that he wanted a third wife. He consulted his first wife and she suggested that he marry a woman whom she knew—a single mother with four children. Shafeeq agreed and, in so doing, felt he was doing something charitable: "Paying somebody's bills is really a big deal in the 'hood when you're dealing with African-American women." The truth was, he said, there just weren't enough responsible African-American fathers and husbands to go around. "If you can get one man who's going to help the children—be there, teach them, give them guidance, leadership, show them how to do it, invest in them—and he does that same thing with another family, some other children, you're duplicating that. You know what I mean? You're Xeroxing righteousness." Shafeeq felt so optimistic about the situation, in fact, that he began "interviewing" women in the hopes of finding a fourth wife.

All of this meant that Shafeeq had a lot riding on his new

business venture. He needed his business to succeed because, say what you will about polygamy, it is not cheap. Aaron didn't know all the details of Shafeeq's situation but he understood what mattered: Shafeeq was desperate to make the whole thing work. Over the course of his investment, Aaron found and used a number of other collection agencies as well, but Shafeeq's agency embodied what he wanted: it was small, scrappy, and a little desperate.

Under the terms of his newly launched fund, Aaron would have to spend the entire investment—all $14 million of it—immediately in order to put his investors' money to work right away. This meant that he needed paper hunters and, inevitably, he turned to the man who had already supplied him with a number of very profitable portfolios: Brandon Wilson. In truth, Brandon was more than just a paper hunter. He also ran his own collection agency in Bangor, Maine; and he maintained a network of buyers, interested in old paper, who would buy Aaron's inventory when he was done with it. Brandon had a checkered past, but whatever he lacked in refinement, he more than compensated for with his knowledge of the industry. Of course, Aaron wouldn't rely on Brandon entirely, but he could make good use of him. Aaron's gut feeling about Brandon was that he was honest and that he knew what he was doing; but it did give him a moment's pause that he was entrusting his fate to a man who may have robbed the very banks for which Aaron, himself, had once worked.

2

THE KING OF CRAP

Brandon and Aaron lived roughly seven hundred miles from each other by car, which is no small distance, but Brandon was a fan of road trips and he periodically made the journey from Bangor to Buffalo. Brandon never drove himself. He preferred to be chauffeured by his driver, Quincy, who worked as a stand-up comic when he wasn't shuttling his boss around. It was always difficult for Aaron to anticipate when, exactly, Brandon would arrive. "If he says he will be here Monday, to visit me in Buffalo," Aaron told me, "I book him for Thursday because he stops at every casino between here and Maine and he shows up with a black eye."

When they met, Aaron would occasionally arrange for them to have dinner or drinks. At Aaron's invitation, one evening, I joined one of their get-togethers at one of Aaron's favorite haunts, the Buffalo Club—a relic from the time when a handful of plutocrats and industrialists ran the city. In 1867, the former president Millard Fillmore helped found the club as a place where like-minded gentlemen could socialize and do business. To call the place stuffy is a spectacular understatement. The interior is a maze of hallways and ballrooms paneled with gleaming wood, lit with chandeliers, and adorned with oil paintings of somber-faced former members who could easily be mistaken for members of a morticians' hall of fame.

Before our dinner, Aaron issued a lengthy disclaimer, warning that Brandon was "rough around the edges," had a "criminal past," and looked like "Uncle Fester on crack." He was an old-school Irishman who had the classic accent of the Boston tough and the personality to match. "I have a lot of trepidation about Brandon, but he will always pay you, unlike Wall Street types who may have a suit and talk nicer, but will hire a lawyer so they don't have to pay you," Aaron said. "I respect Brandon. Going to jail for armed robbery—it's tough to rebound from that."

On our first meeting, and on many subsequent occasions, Aaron and Brandon struck me as a most unlikely duo. Aaron likes to wear two-thousand-dollar custom-made pinstriped suits. He is always well coiffed and perfectly shaven. He strikes a polished and patrician demeanor, right from the moment that he shakes your hand. His sister, Shana, told me, "I always say that you can tell he hasn't worked a manual labor job in his life because his hands are like butter." Aaron is five feet ten, with light brown hair, quick eyes, and soft facial features. "He's always worried about his face looking fat," Shana told me, and for this reason, he regards "cocktails as an acceptable form of dinner."

Brandon, by contrast, favors loose-fitting sports clothing— the style and the brand don't seem to matter, so long as they come with a Red Sox or a Celtics logo. Brandon isn't especially tall, but his chest, shoulders, and neck are hulking. He is overweight, but his wide torso gives you the sense that it is densely packed and would feel like a sack of bricks if you ran into it. With his shaved head, he looks like a bull ready to charge at a moment's notice. When he pulls up his shirt, which he does with some regularity, his arms and upper body are covered with scars, the marks of various knife fights. This is a guy you'd cross the street to avoid.

Upon his arrival at the club, Brandon looked around the place nonchalantly, as if unimpressed. We headed upstairs, where Aaron had reserved a private dining room. As waiters in crisply pressed suits brought us steaks and whiskeys, Brandon held court—talking in his characteristically loud voice, which sounded as if he were shouting at a three-hundred-pound, half-deaf offensive lineman through a megaphone. At first, Brandon spoke mainly about the ins and outs of one of his former lines of work (that is, armed robbery). "We used to wait outside of strip malls for when they'd drop off the night deposit bags, and, in the morning, the first person in would be like the assistant manager of the bank," Brandon said. "The first thing they do, after they open the doors, is they empty the night deposit bags. So we would stand out front with a sledge-hammer and pistol, and when they walked in, one guy would run up and smash through the glass door and make a hole in it and the other one would stick the gun in and say, 'Give me the fucking bags.'"

After spending almost a decade in jail, for several different crimes, Brandon was released in 1998 and took a job as a debt collector. As he recalls, he proved very good at it: "When I first started getting bonus checks, I remember going up to the window at the bank and getting back ten thousand dollars in cash, and I remember thinking, this is better than the days when I actually robbed the bank." Within two years, Brandon had opened his own agency and started working as a debt broker, buying and selling paper. He related the debt market to the drug market: "I used to buy pounds of weed, all right, and then break it down and sell ounces to the other guys who were then breaking it down and selling dime bags on the corner, right? Well, that's what we're doing in debt. I'm buying a national portfolio, right? I'm breaking it down into ounces and I'm selling it in ounces to all these state guys, and then they're turning around, busting a dime, diming it up and getting their money back."

Aaron interrupted his partner with a polite nod of his head: "I'm seeing it from a different perspective. Everybody places a different value on something than anybody else—whether it applies to drugs or whether it applies to debt. So if there is a lawyer in Georgia, and he can buy debt from me for four cents on the dollar and get eight cents back, then he's willing to pay—"

"I'm just relating it to what I know, all right," Brandon interjected. "He can relate it to what he knows. And everybody can relate it to what they know."

"And everybody's making money," said Aaron, winningly.

Aaron explained that it had taken him a while to transition from the buttoned-down banking world to the grimier world of collections. "I worked in the squeaky-clean Bank of America. You go in and everybody went to NYU, Yale, Harvard—the whole fucking nine yards."

Brandon interrupted again, saying that he'd always intended to go to Penn State, but that he is dyslexic and ended up on the bus to the state pen instead. In all seriousness, he added, his time in the state pen enhanced his pedigree in a weird sort of way.

"Part of the package you get of being my business associate or my friend is that I'm gonna protect you from these fucking sharks," he explained. "I'm not gonna let these fucking sharks victimize us because they think they're tough and they think they're scary and they think that no one will do nothing to them. Now, I'm not saying that the reason he"—pausing to point at Aaron—"or other people do business with me is because of that. It's not. Because it very rarely rears its ugly head. But there are a lot of people who do business with me because they know if somebody's double-selling a file or if somebody's fucking up, they know I'm gonna do something about it."

Brandon went on, "If you don't give them a little bit of fear, right—if it's just the law, if it's just the attorney general, if it's just a civil suit—they could care less. So they need someone to go put a stop to that right now. That might not be bashing someone over the head, it might be sitting them down and saying: 'Look, man, you ever do ten years in the can? I have. You ever sat there for ten years waiting for your fucking date? I have. You think you're getting away with this shit? You're not.' That's one way of dealing with it. And then you got people who don't care about that. So okay, then we gotta take it to the street."

And the streets are precisely where Brandon spent much of his youth. His mother, Darlene Wilson, recalls, "At age sixteen I already had two kids and a husband in 'Nam." Brandon was born three years later in 1971. Darlene raised her three kids in and around Boston, including in the notorious housing projects along Mystic Avenue in Somerville, Massachusetts. "Their father was a good man, but he was too young to be [in Vietnam], and he had a hard time transitioning," she said. "It took him about ten years." Raising her children essentially alone in rough neighborhoods, she struggled to keep all of them out of trouble. According to Darlene, during his teenage years—throughout the 1980s—Brandon was always running away from school, getting into fights, selling drugs, and passing through various juvenile delinquent facilities. And she was always on his heels: "When he was growing up, I was chasing Brandon around the projects with a bat, and he was throwing stones at me, and I was hitting the stones back at him with the bat—but boy, could he run. He was a runner. He didn't want to come home. His father was going to kick his butt—his uncles, too— but you couldn't find him. He was like an imaginary person. A ghost."

What made this more frustrating, Darlene says, is that he was so smart. "I had Brandon, I guess you would call it 'tested,' when he was three, and he was highly intelligent," she told me. "It was at Harvard University—they had a baby clinic—and they said that his brain went faster than everyone else's. He was always a wiseass, always smarter than everybody else." Although Brandon had never really attended high school, years later, when he was in prison, an official noted in his records that his "assessment scores" indicated that he read at the "highest levels" and that he should start attending "college level classes." Darlene says that she sensed this potential all along and that—much like Herb Siegel, who had such high hopes for his son—she "expected great things" from Brandon.

It's hard to know what exactly derailed Brandon, but drugs were almost certainly part of the problem. Both of Brandon's siblings struggled with addiction before dying young; and according to his prison records, Brandon was using marijuana by the age of twelve and cocaine and angel dust by fourteen. He ran with a pack of kids who were always getting into trouble. His future wife, Sharon—who knew him since he was roughly thirteen years old—says that, even back then, he was "the leader of his little pack" and that all the kids followed him around and took orders from him. "He wasn't a good kid, but he *was* a good kid," she told me, explaining that he would break the law constantly but that he was never a bully and would always stick up for the underdog.

Brandon spent much of his youth in custody as a ward of the state's Department of Youth Services (DYS), but he proved masterful at escaping from their facilities—and from the police—time and time again. Darlene, who kept a detailed journal for years, chronicled his escapes. In February 1986, she wrote that Brandon had run away and had been missing from DYS for ten weeks. At the time, he was fourteen years old. "I feel that the system has failed my son in all respects," she concluded in her journal. "I have fought tooth and nail to get help for my son, or just to get someone to care what happens to him other than me. No luck." Often months would go by and she wouldn't know where he was, until she received word that he was locked up once again. On one occasion, she learned that he was being held at a facility in Springfield, Massachusetts, only when she received a medical bill for the treatment of his broken knuckles.

Often, in her hastily scrawled journal entries, you can sense Darlene's desperation. "Brandon is acting weird again," she wrote in May 1988, when Brandon was sixteen. "I think he is back on the shit." A month later, in June, she wrote that she believed he was "on the pipe" and that she had "taken out the warrant for him," but had no sense of when or where he would turn up. In July, she wrote that the police had found him: "They caught him with crack! Oh God! Help him." A day later: "DYS just called. Some girl named Debbie called to say Brandon ran!" A week after that, Darlene drove around looking for him, searching the projects and lamenting that he was "nowhere to be found" and "yet you know he's there!" Eventually, she received word that the police had him in custody and that they had beaten him thoroughly. Her only desire, throughout all of this, she says, was to get "the devil" out of him and spring him from his "self-inflicted hell."

Darlene also wrote about how, at various times, she relied on Brandon for help: "Big turnaround for Brandon and for me. This past weekend he had to bail me out of jail for a change! Poor kid! And poor me! Right? Well, I certainly can't say that I didn't know better. 'O.U.I.' they call it—operating under the influence . . . A.A. here I come. Brandon has been calling me every day to give me pep talks, telling me to read certain pages of the Big Book."

By the time he was in his early twenties, Brandon had amassed a criminal record that read like the footnotes to an academic article. His many offenses included trespassing, assault and battery, knowingly receiving stolen property, armed robbery (three counts), possession of mace, larceny, armed assault in a home (two counts), reckless driving, operating under the influence, and—for good measure—swimming in a restricted area. An attempt to rob a vault ended in a high-speed car chase and a spectacular crash. And these, of course, were only the times he was caught. He was never busted for robbing night deposit boxes or toy stores, both of which he claimed to have done repeatedly.

While in prison, Brandon didn't break his stride. His prison records indicate that he gambled, smoked marijuana, fought other inmates, and kept a dirty and cluttered cell—one of his jailers once noted an "open can of tuna fish dumped out on the floor." These infractions repeatedly landed him in solitary confinement. "He was viewed as a management problem," one report notes. "He was suspected of strong-arming other inmates and possible drug dealing." He also appears to have tolerated no disrespect from his fellow inmates, and prison records indicate that he "assaulted another inmate during the course of a game of Monopoly." The dispute, as Brandon recalls it, began on the opening roll of the game when one of the players landed on a property, bought it, and demanded to put up a hotel. "You can't buy a hotel until you have all three properties," Brandon told him. The man—whom Brandon described as a steroid-using, muscle-bound racist with lightning bolts tattooed on each arm—then called Brandon a "p.c. punk." The *p.c.* stood for "protective custody," which is where a prisoner was sent if he was a "rat." This was the gravest of insults. According to his records, Brandon proceeded to beat the man with his fists.

On another occasion, his records note that he refused to vacate the prison yard and told a guard: "Call your boys, I don't give a fuck—you don't scare me." This landed Brandon in solitary confinement for five days, and, while there, he says he passed the time by reading all day long and into the night in the dim light of the moon. His favorite books were the Louis L'Amour westerns about the open plains of Texas.

When he was finally released, in 1998, he moved in with Sharon at her house in Medford, Massachusetts. Brandon started working in construction, building concrete forms for the foundations of houses. One day, he bumped into the sister of an old friend who told him, "Brandon, you are too smart to be doing this. Look at this . . ." She pulled out a bonus check for $3,500 that she had earned as a debt collector. "As soon as she showed it to me, I said to myself, *If this airhead dingbat could make that, I got to get down there, because wait until they get a load of me.* You got to understand, there was a time when I would have strangled you for thirty-five hundred dollars."

One of Brandon's first jobs in collections was at a law firm in Boston that had two divisions, one composed of collectors stationed at phone banks and the other manned by lawyers who sued debtors in court. Brandon was appalled by how the office worked. "There was a lot of crooked stuff going on," he told me. "I noticed it right away and I put a stop to it." Typically, in collection agencies, collectors earn bonuses by hitting various targets each month—say, a certain number of dollars collected. The top earner on any given month is often given an additional bonus. Brandon noticed that the manager was gaming the system, moving cash from one collector's account to another's, so that a certain collector could hit his target and be the agency's top earner. In this scam, his collector would get paid and then give a kickback to the manager. There were other scams as well, and they all offended Brandon: "Without any hook or crook, I'm putting up fifty grand a month, and then you got these guys that are stealing, putting up eighty, making me look like I'm not the best." Brandon immediately confronted the manager. "I literally went over to the guy and said, 'Look, next time you do that, have your hands up because you're taking money out of my kid's mouth, and I'm not going to let you do it!'"

The scamming stopped.

It wasn't long before Brandon's abilities as a collector, combined with his efforts to clean up the office, caught the attention of one of the firm's owners, a well-regarded lawyer named Jeff Schreiber. On their first encounter, Brandon introduced himself—much as he subsequently introduced himself to Aaron Siegel—by explaining that he was a former armed robber who did "ten years in the can." Jeff was not impressed. "He made me cringe when he told me about going to prison [and that] he's a convicted felon," Jeff told me. "I thought, *Oh great, this is what I have on my payroll.*" And yet that didn't stop Jeff from soon promoting Brandon to become a manager. He was impressed that Brandon learned the business so quickly, could do complicated math in his head, and had good leadership skills.

Jeff told me that working in collections taught him to look beyond people's appearances. He lost roughly a million dollars when he bought phony debt from a scam artist who seemed to be the very embodiment of respectability, a millionaire with a large home in Greenwich, Connecticut, and an endowed chair in his family's name at a prominent university. Brandon was precisely the opposite: an apparent criminal whom you could count on. In fact, years later, when Brandon needed a letter of reference, Jeff described him as a "real life Horatio Alger story."

During his time at Schreiber's law firm, Brandon would periodically receive calls from debtors who wanted to pay off debts that did not appear to be in the firm's computer system. Eventually, he discovered that these accounts were being stored in a gigantic file with tens of thousands of older accounts on which the statute of limitations had expired. In Massachusetts, the statute of limitations on credit-card debt is six years. This means that when a debtor stops paying his or her bills, a creditor has exactly six years to file suit against him or her to retrieve its money. After this, debtors are safe from being sued. Many professionals in collections assume that such "out-of-stat" accounts are worthless, but Brandon quickly saw an opportunity. Some of these debtors clearly wanted to pay, which is why they had gone to the trouble of contacting the original creditor, and subsequently gotten in touch with him. As hardened and cynical as Brandon was, he clung to a belief that most people essentially wanted to do the honorable thing and pay what they owed. It was just a question of whether they could.

Several years later, in 2003—when Brandon was running his own ten-man shop in Middleborough, Massachusetts—he received a phone call from the co-owner of a large agency where he had once worked. The man, whom I will call Madison, explained that he was embroiled in a heated legal battle with his partner over control of the agency and its assets. Madison was short on cash, and he asked Brandon if he would be interested in covertly trying to collect on a file of roughly 100,000 accounts, the vast majority of which were out-of-stat. The obvious question was: Whose accounts were these? According to Brandon, the answer was unclear. Madison's agency was funded by a number of investors, and at one time the accounts belonged to them; yet because the accounts were so old, they had essentially been forgotten. Madison suspected that someone *might* be able to collect on them, and that's why he called Brandon. They made a tentative deal: Brandon would work the accounts and keep a percentage, or a contingency fee, on whatever he collected and give the rest to Madison. Within a month, Brandon and his employees had collected $180,000, a fact that he kept to himself. When Madison checked back in on him, Brandon offered him $100,000 in a brown paper bag to buy the accounts outright. Madison, who needed the cash, agreed. In the year that followed, Brandon says that he earned roughly $1 million from Madison's 100,000 out-of-stat accounts and then, amazingly, sold all of the remaining accounts—the ones he couldn't collect on—for more than what he paid for the original file.

In addition to collecting on debt, Brandon began buying and selling it as well. He talked to everyone, did his research, and found opportunities that no one else could—like a portfolio of paper that no one had touched for five years, other than an incompetent call center based in Brazil. "I am a bottom feeder," Brandon told me. "I specialize in finding paper that everyone else thinks is worthless." As far as Brandon was concerned, the older and more beaten-up that debt *appeared* to be, the better. People falsely assumed that it was very difficult to collect on old debt, but it all depended on the history of the portfolio—who exactly had tried to collect on it, how long they had been trying, and how successful they had been. Brandon's specialty became finding old debt that paid. "I buy old crap," Brandon told me. "I'm the King of Crap."

Brandon's main problem was that he spent money as quickly as he made it. This meant that he often required capital to finance his deals. Aaron was precisely what he needed—a man of means who had the sophistication and polish to court investors with deep pockets. The fact that Aaron had $14 million to spend in the summer of 2008 was very good news for Brandon.

There was, however, a catch.

Aaron now wanted to buy paper directly from Brandon's sources, without relying on him as an intermediary. In the past, when Aaron owned and operated his own collection agency, he would simply buy the paper from Brandon—without knowing all of the details of where Brandon had purchased his paper or how much he had purchased it for. This had worked out well for Brandon. In fact, as Brandon told me, he often bought paper for one penny on the dollar and then immediately sold it to Aaron for two pennies on the dollar, thus doubling his money instantly. Aaron now wanted more transparency and more control. He wanted Brandon to reveal all of his suppliers, help him analyze all prospective deals, and then effectively step aside and let Aaron make the deals directly. In return, Aaron would offer Brandon a 5-percent commission on all of the purchases that he made from Brandon's sources.

In theory, this new arrangement meant that Brandon stood to make a lot of money. Aaron had $14 million to spend, and since he was also authorized to reinvest his profits for a limited time, it was likely that Aaron would be purchasing more than $20 million worth of paper. If Brandon brokered all of these deals, he could make $1 million. He also stood to make an additional 5-percent commission selling all of the accounts that the agencies Aaron hired did not collect on. Despite all of this, Brandon had reservations. The deal meant changing his business model, trusting Aaron, and relinquishing a way of doing business—going all the way back to his days as a criminal—in which you never, ever gave up your sources or suppliers. In the end, Brandon agreed, but not without some misgivings. As Brandon told me: "I feel like I sold out to the corporate suits for five percent. At first, I was like: *Fuck you, I am not giving you my sources or my prices—that is how I feed my family.* But I did it to make a million bucks."

From the very first evening that I spent with them, at the Buffalo Club, I began to glean that the core of their relationship was a mutual curiosity, distrust, and need. They were two men, roughly the same age, from vastly different backgrounds. Each of them was deeply fascinated by the other's world. Neither of them was so naïve as to trust the other fully. As Aaron put it, "I love Brandon, but if you give him an inch, he'll take a mile. Any time you show vulnerability—like, 'Hey I need you' or 'Thank you, you really helped me out'—he'll push it as far as he can go." Collections isn't "a gentleman's game," he concluded, and "Brandon is one of the best at it."

At the end of the day, however, they needed each other. Indeed, as our dinner at the Buffalo Club drew to a close, Brandon returned again and again to his credo: no matter how smart you were and no matter how many good deals you found, sometimes the only person who could check the thieves in the collection business was "somebody who actually fucking threatened them." Brandon paused, went into character, and then barked, "*Do it again and I'll break your fucking nose.*"

"It's very much an alpha-male-type thing, wouldn't you say?" asked Aaron admiringly.

"Right," said Brandon. "And they don't really know, *Will he actually punch me in the nose if I . . .*" Brandon nodded his head convincingly. "Yeah, I would. Yeah, I would."

"You do prefer conversation first," suggested Aaron.

"Correct, absolutely," said Brandon. "And at the end of that conversation, if you still persist, I will still punch you in the nose."

"How do you deal with the women?" asked Aaron.

"No, but listen, I wouldn't punch you in the nose for doing anything other than something criminal. Like just because you were good at your job? No, I don't walk around threatening you."

"No, you're more of an uplifting guy," Aaron offered.

"Right," said Brandon. "I'm a motivator."

3

THE PACKAGE

If Aaron had doubts about his partnership with Brandon, they were soon dispelled. Brandon quickly began proving his worth—sniffing out inefficiencies in the marketplace like a bloodhound chasing the faintest of scents. By the fall of 2008, Brandon was increasingly interested in a large debt buyer based in Painesville, Ohio, known as Hudson & Keyse. Brandon had been buying paper from Hudson & Keyse for several years, but he had recently noticed that the price of the paper was getting cheaper; meanwhile, rather counterintuitively, the quality of the paper remained high and, in some cases, seemed to be improving. Brandon suspected that the company was in financial trouble—and he was right. An insider at Hudson & Keyse later told me, "There was a desperation to sell paper to raise funds." At Brandon's urging, Aaron capitalized on this desperation. On December 16, 2008, Aaron purchased a parcel of debt from Hudson & Keyse containing 8,518 accounts. The parcel had a "face value" of $47.5 million and Aaron agreed to buy it for precisely one penny on the dollar.

The portfolio of debt that Aaron purchased—which I will refer to simply as "the Package"—was the archetype of the kind of paper that Aaron hoped to buy. The Package quickly proved to be "solid gold," as Aaron put it. In his estimation, the people at Hudson & Keyse were "total idiots" for parting with it so cheaply: "They left too much meat on the bone." In fact, Aaron soon went back to Hudson & Keyse looking for more, and began buying similar portfolios on a monthly basis in an arrangement known as a "forward-flow agreement." This was, for Aaron, the start of a very profitable relationship.

The Package itself was composed of credit-card debts from a range of original creditors including Bank of America, Washington Mutual, Huntington National Bank, Unity One Federal Credit Union, and many others. Most of the accounts had likely been sold at least once before; and many had probably been sold multiple times. The debtors in the Package hailed from a range of locales across the country, including Ewa Beach (Hawaii), Dutch Harbor (Alaska), Prairie Village (Kansas), and Rock Springs (Wyoming). Some of these debtors owed as much as $29,777 and others as little as $209; some were as young as nineteen, others were as old as eighty-five; some had accounts that had been charged off by the banks as long ago as 1989, others had accounts charged off as recently as 2008. All of their fates were now bound together in the form of a single Microsoft Excel spreadsheet that had been sold to Aaron for one penny on the dollar.

Debtor #2,991 in the Package was a single mom named Joanna who lived in the suburbs of a large Midwestern city. In 2006, Joanna ran for her life, literally. She fled the home of her abusive ex-boyfriend, who had tried his best to kill her, once even pushing her out of a moving car. She left with their one-year-old daughter in tow, and hunkered down in a small apartment. From the start, it was rocky. Joanna often lived week to week, not knowing how she would pay her bills or put food on the table. She took whatever jobs she could find, and often two at a time. For a while, she worked weekdays as a nanny and then spent weekends doing back-to-back eight-hour shifts as a certified nurse's assistant at an assisted living facility. She rushed through a frantic routine, as if her own personal needs were just another set of bills that she didn't have the time or resources to confront.

To save money, Joanna grew accustomed to wearing the same clothing, year after year, even though her socks and her underwear became faded, threadbare, and torn with holes. As her daughter grew up, Joanna paid for her to take tae kwon do and gymnastics classes. Joanna helped her with homework and took her to the library often. At night, Joanna would clean her apartment, do the laundry, and when the last chore was done—and there was nothing to do but sit and catch her breath—she worried about her debt. Over the previous thirteen years, Joanna had accumulated considerable credit-card debt on her Washington Mutual card. Part of the debt was hers and she bore full responsibility for it; part of it, however, was the doing of her abusive ex-boyfriend. Throughout their relationship, he was periodically unemployed; and, during these times, Joanna used her credit card to pay for things. So did he. According to Joanna, he often used it to cover repairs on his car or, as she recalls it, to "soup up" his computer because he loved to play online games. "He was buying stuff without me even knowing it," said Joanna. She confronted him but said, if she pushed too hard, he "clobbered" her. "I try not to live in regret," Joanna told me, "but he screwed me mentally, emotionally, physically, and [now] financially."

Throughout the fall of 2006, Joanna's bank records show

that she was trying to pay off her balance and making no further purchases on the card. In September she paid $83, in October she paid $85, in November she paid $39. At this point, she owed Washington Mutual $2,712. After that, she simply stopped paying what she owed. It was not a responsible thing to do, but Joanna says that cash was scarce and she had to pick and choose which of her bills to pay. Meanwhile, the interest continued to accumulate, at a rate of 24 percent; and, by June 2007, she owed $3,206. Joanna didn't take any of this lightly. She was and is determined to fix her credit—in large part because she fears it may handicap her daughter. "I don't know how it works," she admitted to me, "but I don't want my bad credit to reflect badly on my daughter. Let's just say she's smart enough to get a scholarship of some sort and they're like, *No— because your mom is not good enough . . .*"

In the ensuing years, Joanna received calls from numerous debt collectors about her Washington Mutual card; and then, one day in 2009, she received a call from someone who presented himself as an "officer of the court." "He said, 'You need to call me back as soon as you can because they have filed a lawsuit against you and you're going to be arrested and brought to court for this outstanding balance.'" Joanna immediately went into a panic. "I thought, *My God, I'm going to go to jail. Who's going to take care of my daughter?*" This threat wasn't as outlandish as it sounds. As of 2010, more than a third of all states permitted the jailing of consumers for failing to pay a debt.

Joanna called the collector right away and explained that, currently, she had just three hundred dollars in her bank account. The collector said that she owed much more than this, but that he would settle for a onetime payment of three hundred. Looking back, this whole exchange seems odd to Joanna, but at the time, she felt so desperate and panicked that she readily acquiesced. This left her with no cash. She borrowed fifty dollars from her brother, and another hundred from her parents, so she could afford gas and groceries for the next two weeks. To save money, Joanna lived on a strict diet of peanut-butter-and-jelly sandwiches. Meanwhile, she never heard back from these collectors, nor did she ever receive a receipt or any kind of confirmation in the mail from them. Little did she know it, but the people who'd called her were collecting on stolen paper—debt that belonged to Aaron but which, somehow or another, had been pilfered from him.

Roughly a thousand miles away, in a small town in the Southwest, debtor #3,159 from the Package—a woman named Theresa—was facing problems of her own. Theresa defies almost all the stereotypes of debtors. She joined the U.S. Marines in the early 1990s, at the age of eighteen, and served for the next eight years. Years later, she still talks like a marine, answering all my questions with a "Yes, sir." Theresa was so determined to live responsibly that, throughout much of her teens, she worked more than thirty hours a week at McDonald's, earning $4.25 an hour. She saved almost everything she made. When her father lost his job and her parents fell behind on their mortgage payments, Theresa—who was still in high school at the time—bailed them out by giving them the $2,000 that they needed to avert foreclosure. When I asked her how she juggled so much at such a young age, she replied, "Well, I didn't come from people with money, sir, and I knew that I had to handle my own business." Theresa was resolved to pull herself up into the ranks of the middle class and, upon joining the Marines, the very first thing that she did was open a 401(k) retirement plan.

After eight years of service, Theresa got married and settled down into a comfortable middle-class existence. She took a job as the manager of a restaurant and, later on, of a grocery store.

Together, she and her husband were making roughly $90,000 a year. They had acquired some credit-card debt—a few thousand dollars' worth—but they were paying it off consistently in installments of roughly $180 a month. Theresa didn't like having that debt, but it seemed manageable. At that time, life in general seemed manageable—and that's precisely when everything fell apart.

It started at the grocery store, when someone stole her cell phone. Theresa hurried home to call T-Mobile, asking them to activate the chip in her old cell phone. But there was a mix-up, and instead of routing all of *her* calls to this phone, T-Mobile began routing all of her *husband's* calls to the phone. Right away, Theresa received a voice mail that was intended for her husband. The message was short but startling: "I took a shower and I'm waiting for you to come over."

"What happened was, I found out that my husband of eleven years had another family somewhere else," she told me matter-of-factly. "He had a girlfriend and a four-year-old that he had been supporting without me knowing." Theresa filed for divorce in 2005, but this quickly created a fresh set of problems. "He left me with everything except the truck that he took, and that was fine, except that I now had to pay for everything," she explained. "I had the credit-card debt. I had the mortgage. I had everything." Meanwhile, she went from having a dual income of $90,000 to a lone income of roughly $50,000.

As the direness of her situation became increasingly evident, Theresa got a roommate and eventually took a second job. It still wasn't enough to cover her bills, however, so she went into triage mode. She would pay her mortgage first, then the monthly bill for her vehicle, then her utilities, and then she would deal with everything else. At the time, she says she had four credit cards—which was close to the national average of

3.5 cards per person. The balances on these cards, she says, reflected both the debt from her married days and new debt that she had incurred to pay for groceries and "other staples" when it got tight. Theresa soon realized, however, that she could not even begin to pay all of her credit-card bills each month, so she made a decision—a bad one, it turns out—to stop paying some of the cards altogether. She opted to keep paying two of them, including her Washington Mutual card. "I don't remember how I made that decision," she told me uncomfortably. "It was kind of a bad time." In July 2006, she owed $4,184 to Washington Mutual. In August, September, and October she continued making steady payments even though she wasn't using the card to make any purchases.

Theresa's decision not to pay her other credit cards proved to be very shortsighted; it had an immediate effect on her credit rating, and, as a result, the interest rate on the two cards that she was paying skyrocketed to the uppermost legal limit, which was just under 30 percent. Theresa tried to keep making payments, but often they were late, triggering more fees. Between January 2006 and April 2007 she incurred eight late fees of $39 each. During this same period, she also came to owe another $817 in interest. The interest, combined with late fees, caused her to go over her credit limit—which, in turn, triggered an over-the-limit fee. Eventually, Theresa stopped paying her Washington Mutual bill altogether because she says she couldn't even afford the minimum payments.

"They probably would've gotten a lot more money from me if they would have left me at my original twelve to thirteen percent interest rate and worked with me a little bit," says Theresa. "But what happened was, when they saw me starting to fail, they jacked it up to twenty-nine percent. I guess they were trying to get whatever they could before I went completely under. Well, what happened was they actually pushed me under."

In March 2007, Theresa finally got a much-needed break: drawing on her experience in the Marines, she landed a job with the federal government as a Border Patrol agent. As a matter of policy, the U.S. Border Patrol says that debts and "financial issues" may render candidates "unsuitable" for service. Theresa says that initially, when she joined the Border Patrol, her superiors understood her predicament and were sympathetic. "They could see I was working two jobs, I had a roommate, and I could put everything on paper to justify why, at that point, my credit was a mess." But that would not work indefinitely. Theresa knew that in five years she would be required to undergo a new background check and that she likely wouldn't be able to justify having such poor credit. The bottom line was that she needed to pay off at least some of her outstanding debts as soon as possible.

The situation came to a head in 2009 when she began receiving phone calls about her Washington Mutual card from people who claimed to work at a law firm. Like Joanna, she was told that unless she paid off the balance in full, they would take her to court. Theresa worried that such a lawsuit could destroy her career as a federal law enforcement officer. The collectors explained that she now owed more than $6,000, with interest, but they offered her a deal in which she could settle the matter for just $2,700. Theresa says that she set up a payment plan and, over the course of the next six months, the money was withdrawn directly from her checking account.

Despite everything she had been through, Theresa felt pretty good about the situation. She had finally paid off a fairly substantial debt. There was just one problem: the company never sent a letter to her confirming that she had paid the bill. And, what's worse, the payment never appeared on her credit report. She spent the next six months trying to understand where, exactly, her money had gone. "I didn't want the money back," she told me. "I just wanted somebody to say, 'Hey, she tried to pay.'" At the time, she was trying to land a new job as a customs agent. "And they're coming to me [and asking], 'How come you got so much debt?' And I'm trying to say, 'Hey, I paid it. I paid it.' But I didn't have any proof." In the meantime, her credit report would continue to indicate that she had *not* paid this debt, which meant—among other things—that she would likely have to pay more for a car loan, a mortgage, or insurance.

"I didn't know who to turn to for resources," she told me. "I couldn't get my money back, and I kept running into dead ends everywhere." All of this led her to conclude wearily: "There are a thousand ways to rip off desperate people. The more desperate you are, and the less you have, the easier it is."

It wasn't an accident that Theresa's and Joanna's debts ended up in the hands of thieves. When the original creditor, Washington Mutual, sold their debts it stopped caring about what Theresa and Joanna owed, how they were treated, or the fate of their personal information. The banks' contracts testify to this indifference. For example, in a series of transactions in 2009 and 2010, Bank of America sold millions of dollars of charged-off debt to a company in Denver called CACH LLC. In the sales agreement, Bank of America said that it would *not* make "any representations, warranties, promises, covenants, agreements, or guaranties of any kind or character whatsoever" about the accuracy of the accounts it was selling. When Aaron bought the Package from Hudson & Keyse, the contract of sale had similar wording. It stated, for example, that the seller was offering no "warranty of any kind" relating to the "validity, accuracy, or sufficiency of information" that was being sold. In other words, there might be problems with the debts, but they were simply being sold on *as is*.

And there were problems, dating right back to the original creditor, Washington Mutual. For both Joanna and Theresa, bank records confirm that Washington Mutual issued them significant credits—$456 for Joanna and $701 for Theresa—on the very same day that it sold their debts. It's unclear what the credits were for. An official at Chase Bank, which acquired Washington Mutual in 2008, speculates that the credits may have been offered as relief—gifts, essentially. On their monthly statements, the credits appeared as payments alongside the words "PAYMENT RECEIVED—THANK YOU." Whatever the explanation, one thing is certain: when Aaron purchased these accounts, in 2008, neither Joanna's nor Theresa's balance reflected these credits. Somewhere along the way, quite possibly at the bank itself, they were simply forgotten or ignored. Such sloppy record keeping may seem surprising, but it is prevalent enough that, in 2009, the Federal Trade Commission (FTC) stated in a report: "When accounts are transferred to debt collectors, the accompanying information often is so deficient that the collectors seek payment from the wrong consumer or demand the wrong amount from the correct consumer."

In truth, there was little that Theresa or Joanna could do; they had paid off their debts to the wrong collectors and fallen into the debt underworld. If anyone were going to help them, it wouldn't be the state attorney general, or the Better Business Bureau, or the FTC, or even the police, but the former banker and the former armed robber who had bought their debts.

4

BAD PAPER

One of Aaron's most persistent and anxiety-provoking concerns was that a dishonest collector or debt broker might swindle him. In the fall of 2009, this fear appeared to become a reality. Around the same time that Theresa and Joanna were getting phone calls from a mysterious law firm, Aaron received an e-mail from the owner of one of the agencies that he hired to do his collecting. The collectors at this agency were getting the same message from numerous debtors: We just paid off these accounts—*to someone else.*

At the time, Aaron had no idea exactly how many accounts had been compromised. What he did know was that somehow, someone else had gotten access to his files and was collecting on them. Aaron was puzzled. Was this the work of a renegade collector within one of his agencies who was collecting on his own and pocketing the cash? Was it possible that someone had stolen these files or somehow managed to copy them? Whatever the explanation, Aaron needed to deal with the situation quickly.

On several previous occasions, he had dealt with collection agencies that had tried to cheat him in one fashion or another. In one instance, he recalled placing a portfolio with a married couple that ran an agency in Florida. For several months the agency sent him good returns, and then suddenly, the payments stopped. "Oh boy," Aaron recalled. "It comes through the grapevine that, apparently, the wife developed a crack cocaine addiction. She sold all the files out from under him—or stole all of them—and ran off with the money. And that was that." Aaron says he had no recourse. "I could sue her. Totally worthwhile to sue a crackhead, right? What am I going to do with that? I'm gonna throw good money after bad."

On another occasion, Aaron says that he bought a file for $100,000 from two Buffalo-based debt brokers. The paper was supposed to be "fresh," directly from HSBC, only it wasn't. In fact, it was fairly worthless. He recalled going to the local district attorney—who was actually an acquaintance of his—but the case proved a hard sell. It was difficult for Aaron to explain all of the nuances of the deal and, by the time he had, he says it became apparent to him that the district attorney had plenty of cases that would be easier to prosecute. "They're in the business of picking the low-hanging fruit," said Aaron. "And that's not a knock on them." Aaron concluded that he had to fend for himself. "This is the Wild West," he explained. "You're buying and selling Excel files, and everybody—even the very best—gets burned."

After going to the district attorney on the HSBC matter, Aaron hired a lawyer at one of Buffalo's most prestigious law firms and sued the debt brokers who had cheated him. The process dragged on for almost two years, and at one point I tagged along with Aaron when he visited his lawyer's office to get an update on the status of the litigation. The lawyer—a

young, handsome fellow who was sharply dressed in a crisp
white shirt and a pink-and-yellow striped tie—relayed to us
what he had discovered. As it turns out, the two brokers who
sold the debt to Aaron didn't actually own it. The lawyer had
obtained a judgment against the two brokers' companies, which
seemed like good news, but it wasn't. "At this point, it is clear
that the companies are shells," the lawyer said. The addresses
were no longer even valid. "The individuals are deadbeats. So
just because you get a judgment doesn't mean you can collect
it." Aaron could press on, but the defendants were stalling and
had failed to show up in court on three separate occasions.

"They know that this is costing me money!" Aaron fumed.
"It is the same tactic debtors use—*call me back tomorrow*. It is
the same exact tactic."

Ultimately, the lawyer told Aaron that he shouldn't be too
hopeful or expect to recoup what he had lost.

"At the end of the day it was a big circle jerk?" asked Aaron.

"Yes," replied the lawyer.

It was this experience, and others like it, that shook Aaron's
faith in the regulators and the judicial system. And so, when he
heard that someone else was trying to collect on *his* accounts,
he picked up the phone and called his fixer, Brandon, for ad-
vice. Brandon was committed to helping Aaron because he had
pledged, long ago, to keep the "sharks" at bay. What's more,
Brandon was in the process of selling some of the paper that
appeared to be affected and, unless he resolved this matter, he
would lose his commissions.

As soon as he got the call from Aaron, Brandon started with
his detective work. First, he needed to match the fraud to individual accounts. So he spoke with the owner of the collection
agency who worked for Aaron—the one who first identified the
problem—and asked him for the phone numbers of all the

debtors who had recently paid this mysterious other agency. Then, one by one, Brandon began contacting these debtors. None of them could recall the name of the mystery agency, but several combed through their most recent credit-card statements and identified the company that had processed the payments they had made. Brandon called the processing company. "So I got them on the phone, told them that *I* was the debtor, and said, 'What the fuck is this? I am reversing the charge! What company charged me for this?'" And, like that, Brandon had the name and phone number of the collection agency.

"I called up the agency and introduced myself as the debtor," he said. "The woman on the other end of the phone tells me, 'You are being sued, you better pay!' I said, 'First, give me your address.' She is like, 'I am not giving you the address.'" Brandon called back, and this time he got a man who claimed to be the owner of the agency. Brandon told him, "You guys are stealing money." The owner of the agency, who asked to be identified only by his nickname—Bill—insisted that the accounts were his. In the coming days, Bill received a series of threatening calls and voice mails from Brandon. "I started getting these calls from this Boston cat with this real big Boston accent," Bill told me. He spoke "like he was a gangster," said Bill, and threatened to "come to my office, kick over my computers, and take my server." Bill refused to stop collecting on the accounts: "I let him know what it was [like] in this city and if he came here, [talking] like this, he might not make it out."

After speaking with Bill on the phone—and getting nowhere—Brandon hung up and glanced around his office in Bangor, surveying the faces of his collectors. He called out the names of four of them. They all stood up without questions. One was a young employee named Jeremy Mountain; as he recalls it, Brandon calmly explained to them what they were about to do: "We're gonna shut down this rogue agency or burn it down to the ground." No one hesitated. They all piled into Brandon's small Mercedes sports car and drove more than six hundred miles to Buffalo. "On average, the guys in the car weighed about two hundred forty pounds," Jeremy said. "I was the only person who hadn't gone to prison."

Before "going to war," as Brandon put it, he and his crew stopped by Aaron's office in Buffalo. As it turns out, Brandon had some business to settle with Aaron as well. Under their arrangement, Aaron was supposed to notify Brandon every time that he purchased paper from one of Brandon's sources, and then send him a 5-percent commission. Brandon suspected that Aaron had either forgotten or simply neglected to pay him for some of these deals. In the car, Brandon apprised his posse of the situation: "I told my guys, 'I know he has been holding out.'" One of the men in the car recalled Brandon vowing to them, "We are not walking out without a check." Brandon figured that now was the perfect time to leverage his position and demand payment.

Aaron's then-deputy—whom I will call Lilly to protect her privacy—recalled Brandon's arrival vividly. "He showed up in the office in a long black coat, drinking whiskey out of the bottle, with all these guys that I would not want to meet in a dark alley," she said. Brandon's arrival also made a lasting impression on Aaron. "They come down here in this small Mercedes, and they come storming out of it like clowns out of a clown car—only they're ex-cons." With some trepidation, Aaron invited them up to his office. "One guy was this scary son of a bitch," Aaron said, and, upon entering his office, he stopped to stare at a picture of Aaron's wife. "He had these piercing eyes, and he is like, 'Your wife is very pretty.' And I'm thinking, *He is going to murder my wife.*"

As far as Aaron was concerned, Brandon's visit was hardly

comforting. "It doesn't give me any peace of mind," he told me. "It just ratchets up your level of stress. All of a sudden, you're swimming in waters you didn't really want to swim in, never would have conceived you would be swimming in, right? I feel good that I was able to—in some instances, through Brandon's persuasion—protect my investors' money better than I would have been able to otherwise. But really? This is what I'm doing? It makes for an entertaining story. But would you want to do it? Would you switch places with me?"

On this visit, Aaron quickly resolved the matter of the unpaid commissions by writing Brandon a check for $50,000. He sent him another check, for $117,000, several days later. And at Brandon's urging, Aaron also paid each member of Brandon's posse $500 for their time and services. After visiting Aaron's offices, Brandon and his associates set to work, piling back into his Mercedes. Brandon placed a call to Shafeeq, the Muslim debt collector whose agency Aaron had hired and co-owned. Brandon and Shafeeq weren't friends exactly, but they were colleagues of a sort—they had known each other for years and had a good rapport. Shafeeq had the advantage of being a local. He knew the collections scene in Buffalo—the good actors, the bad actors, and everybody in between. Shafeeq knew, for example, that Bill owned and operated a corner store near Buffalo's downtown.

There was another benefit to having Shafeeq in the posse as well, namely, that he ran his own security firm and was licensed to carry a firearm. Shafeeq was a stickler for details— like drawing up contracts for the clients whose homes and property he protected. As he told me, "I can go and shoot a person—an intruder, at your house—and it would be a lot easier to do something like that with the security contract in place. Whereas if I'm just showing up at your house, and I shoot somebody, now there's a lot more, you know, paperwork."

Brandon recalls that when they all met up, Shafeeq was wearing a bulletproof vest and had a 9-millimeter pistol with two clips. He also had a machete. Brandon asked him what the knife was for. According to Brandon, Shafeeq's reply was, "It's for when I run out of bullets." When I asked Brandon if anyone else in the Mercedes was armed, he said, "Not legally." Brandon explained that collectors in Buffalo were a rough-and-tumble lot—"there are a lot of shady motherfuckers there"—and he wanted to be ready for the worst.

Brandon and his crew eventually found Bill at his corner store, which he owned and operated in a run-down neighborhood, amid a bleak urban expanse of abandoned storefronts, cracked sidewalks, and empty lots overgrown with weeds. Brandon stepped out of the car and studied the storefront, looking in through the front window, trying to see exactly who was inside. It was hard to tell. Brandon gestured for three of his guys to come with him, including Jeremy and Shafeeq.

Brandon walked into the store and saw an enormous man, roughly six and a half feet tall and 280 pounds. Brandon asked the man his name. It was Bill. The encounter was tense. Jeremy Mountain recalled seeing a gun resting on a shelf behind the checkout counter. Bill confirmed that he had a gun at the ready and recalled that, whether Brandon knew it or not, "he was the one in danger." Brandon looked around. At the back of the store, he saw a door that appeared to lead to a back office. He gestured toward the door and explained, "I don't want an audience." Together the two men walked through the back door, where Brandon hoped they might find some privacy. "Turns out it was a closet," recalled Brandon. "So it's the two of us, just standing there, in a storage closet."

As he remembers it, Brandon told Bill to sit down and then drew close so the two of them were eye to eye. "If you collect one more dollar on this paper," he said, "I will come back down here, I will take your server, I will burn your agency to the ground, I will come to your house and burn it down, and then I will come back here and burn this store down. Understand?" Bill proclaimed his innocence and indignation, insisting that he had bought the file—legitimately—from another debt broker in Buffalo, whom I will identify as Kenny.

This news gave Brandon pause. He knew that Kenny and his associates were notorious in the industry for selling accounts that were stolen or double-sold—meaning the exact same debt had been sold off to two different buyers. Brandon himself had had "a couple of run-ins with these guys" in the past. On one of these occasions, Brandon claimed he was cheated out of money that he was owed and had driven down to Buffalo in order to confront them. He never found them, but he remembered the incident bitterly, and wondered for a second whether what Bill said might be true. For his part, Bill later suggested to me that he mentioned Kenny's name only as a diversion and that—in fact—he had bought the paper from a rogue employee in Aaron's office who was selling the paper covertly and, apparently, illegally.

In any case, at the corner store, Brandon was primarily concerned with impressing upon Bill just how serious and dangerous he was. Shafeeq, who overheard much of their encounter, described it as two "big kids" trying to prove who was meanest: "It was a tough-guy show." Bill says that he refused to be strong-armed and that he told Brandon: "It's not gonna happen here—you're talking to the wrong guy." Brandon was not to be outdone. As Shafeeq recalled it, Brandon went into a tirade, lifting up his shirt and screaming at the top of his lungs, "I got stabbed right here! I got a bullet hole right here!" The tactic worked. "As soon as you see that kind of behavior," said

Shafeeq, "you're like, okay, this dude is absolutely crazy." According to Shafeeq, Bill eventually backed down.

As Brandon saw it, the key now was resolution and so he laid down his terms. Brandon explained to Bill that this entire matter could be resolved quietly without involving the authorities. He issued two demands. The first was that he wanted a spreadsheet documenting the details of every stolen account on which a debtor had made a payment. The second and more important demand: *Stop collecting on all of these accounts and any others that might belong to Aaron.* In the end, Bill made good on his promise to stop collecting on Aaron's accounts. Bill says he was happy to do this because he paid only $10,000 for the accounts and had already collected many times that. What's more, Brandon didn't demand that he return what he had made. "It was a win-win," explained Bill proudly.

The whole episode, however, remained something of a mystery and a mess. In the coming weeks, Bill sent Brandon a series of e-mails in which he continued to maintain that he had purchased the accounts and not stolen them. "We won't be working anything we received or purchased from those guys until this thing gets sorted out," he wrote. What mattered most to Aaron and Brandon was identifying each and every account that Bill's agency had actually collected on. This proved easier said than done. Bill ultimately sent Brandon five separate spreadsheets holding roughly 7,000 accounts, some of which he suspected belonged to Aaron. Of these, more than 2,400 were from the Package. Theresa's and Joanna's names and accounts were on these spreadsheets. This strongly suggests it was Bill's collectors who called the two women, threatened them, and extorted their payments. When I spoke with Bill, he searched through his records, and said he could find no evidence that either Theresa or Joanna had paid him—though he admitted that one of his collectors might have covertly processed their payments and pocketed the money. If they didn't pay Bill's agency, the only other possibility is that some other agency managed to get access to these accounts and collect on them in the same time period.

Aaron resolved to make the best of a bad situation. Whenever he could confirm that a debtor had paid Bill, he closed the account and permanently retired the debt; besides that, there wasn't much more for him to do. For his part, Brandon felt good that the matter was all resolved. In fact, as a thank-you for Bill's prompt and polite cooperation, Brandon says he sent Bill a small present—a trademark Brandon Wilson tiding of goodwill: a file containing one thousand out-of-stat accounts. Brandon speculated that Bill might even become a customer someday but he never heard from him again.

PART TWO

PAPER HUNTERS

5

AARON'S PROBLEM

Recapturing the Package was a victory for Aaron. By taking the law into his own hands, he had avoided the cost and frustration of litigation and minimized his investors' losses. And the Package had been an investment worth protecting. The paper was so good, in fact, that Aaron and Brandon locked up their "forward-flow arrangement" with Hudson & Keyse: the firm continued to sell similar packages to Aaron, each month, until the fall of 2010, when it finally filed for bankruptcy.

If only Aaron could have spent all of his investors' money on paper like this, there's no telling how much he might have made. But it wasn't as simple as that. Aaron had launched the fund in the summer of 2008, and the investors had insisted that he put their money into action. The point of the investment was to make money, and they didn't want it sitting around in a savings account. This meant that Aaron had to buy his paper in bulk, spending the $14 million in the fund right away. Aaron's preferred strategy was for Brandon to identify older, undervalued paper so that Aaron could buy it, work it, and sell it. This was the key to taking advantage of the inefficient market. But these kinds of deals typically weren't available in bulk. Buying the Package, for example, had been a great investment; but it wasn't feasible to replicate this practice on a massive scale. Even Brandon couldn't find that many deals. Not all at once, anyhow.

And so Aaron made a very large and very different purchase, spending roughly $9 million on a portfolio of debt that he bought from Bank of America. He made this deal around the same time that he purchased the Package in late 2008. It was a pivotal deal for Aaron and he proceeded carefully. The bank sent him a sample, almost like a teaser, to give him a sense of the paper that he was about to buy. The paper was "firsts"—no one had worked it other than the bank. And, at 3.5 cents on the dollar, it appeared to be priced well. Aaron analyzed the file, studying the balances, the age of the debt, the regions where the debtors lived, and every other conceivable criterion. Brandon did the same. Brandon was the first to admit that this was outside his realm of expertise. Since he liked to buy older paper, he was less confident buying directly from the bank. Even so, he ultimately concluded that the file looked good. Aaron then negotiated a contract with the bank, demanding that the rest of the paper have the same characteristics as the teaser. He stipulated twenty criteria in the contract—everything from balance size to zip codes. In the end, he felt good about the deal. After all, he was buying this paper from his former employer, Bank of America, one of the nation's leading banks.

There was a problem, however, and it became apparent as soon as Aaron's agencies started collecting on the paper. Almost all the debtors appeared to be elderly, which meant that they generally had less disposable income. Aaron had stipu-

lated many things in the contract, but "date of birth" of debtors was not one of them. "I got a bunch of senior citizens living
on social security," Aaron said. Or, as Brandon put it: "They
fucked us!"

The particulars of the $9 million Bank of America deal re-
mained a source of much hand-wringing and second-guessing
for both Aaron and Brandon. Four years after the fact, I spent
an evening with the two of them and listened to them rehash
the episode so heatedly that it was as if the deal had happened
the previous day. On that occasion, as Brandon worked himself up into one of his tirades, he cursed Bank of America as
a bunch of "scumbags" and yelled, "Even though I was gonna
make a half a million dollars in commission [on the deal], I
said, 'Aaron, I'm really happy right now, but just for the record,
I don't think we should buy this file.'"

"That's not entirely true," Aaron protested. "You looked at
it. Nobody could even give me—"

"I said it's worth the price," Brandon interrupted. "It's good
paper, but we're blowin' all the money on somethin' I don't really
have one hundred percent knowledge on, and I don't know if I
can get my guys to collect on it, because they're used to collecting ten-year-old shit."

When the paper did prove troublesome to collect on, it
wasn't just because the debtors were "a bunch of senior citizens." The other problem was that the economy never really
bounced back. According to the National Bureau of Economic
Research, the recession officially ended in June 2009; but this
was hardly a consolation to the millions of Americans who had
lost their jobs, their homes, and their savings. In fact, several
months later—in October 2009—the unemployment rate peaked
at 10.2 percent, hitting double digits for the first time in twenty-
six years. And by the end of 2009, foreclosure notices had

been sent to some 2.8 million properties in the United States. All of this made it that much tougher for Aaron's agencies to collect.

"In 2006, if people owed ten thousand dollars in credit-card debt, we would push them to refinance their house," Aaron told me. By 2009, "those days were gone," he told me, because "no one had any equity in their homes anymore." Aaron gave an example: "You are an average guy who bought a home for three hundred thousand, and then, during the boom years, the house was suddenly worth five hundred thousand. So you now have two hundred thousand in equity." In those circumstances, Aaron's collectors could encourage debtors to borrow against that equity. But that was then. Now that the real estate bubble had popped, everything had changed. The equity had been lost and, sometimes, the homes, too. "Now you, the debtor, cannot pay back the ten thousand that you owe on your credit card. So what was a friendly discussion before 2007 has become more adversarial now."

After buying the Bank of America paper, Aaron was now doubly committed to acquiring more of the older debt that Brandon specialized in because, as he put it, "We felt like we had to make up ground." And he had the money to do it. As part of Aaron's agreement with his investors, he had the right to reinvest some of their profits for a limited time, and this ultimately gave him at least an additional $6 million to spend on paper. If he bought the right paper cheaply enough, and the economy recovered, he still might do well for his investors. If he didn't, the misguided Bank of America deal might pull him down.

As Aaron struggled to keep his fund profitable, the cumulative stress of his work life and his personal life was taking its toll. By 2009, he was living with his second wife, Andrea, the beautiful brunette whom Herb Siegel had called a "femme fatale." Andrea vacillated between feeling sympathetic and resentful. "I remember him coming home and just looking stressed out," said Andrea. "I would feel bad because I could tell the weight of the world was on his shoulders." Aaron says he worked late and drank heavily, and Andrea complained that, suddenly, she couldn't "get his full attention," whereas once she "never had to ask for it." Like the Mrs. Siegel before her, she had become the wife waiting at home. What really galled her was that when Aaron did come home, they always ended up talking about Brandon. "God, I would hate that," she said. "I feel like when he started working with Brandon is when the wheels came off. I don't know, it just seemed to get [Aaron] into these murky, murky, murky things." He and Brandon would fight "like a married couple," she said. "It reminded me of like this high school relationship between these two idiots that I just wanted to knock both their heads together and say, 'I'm out— you guys should just date.'"

"I wanted to shoot myself in the face," recalled Aaron. "I'm awake at night, I'm drinking way too much, you know, and I'm pulling out my hair because I'm doing something I don't enjoy." One day he asked his deputy, Lilly, to drive him to the hospital because he thought he was having a heart attack. It turned out it was just ulcers—six of them.

The ultimate source of dread for Aaron was his investors and his persistent fear that he might fail them. His biggest investor was a Texas real estate tycoon—whom I will identify only by his first name, John—whose company had developed billions of dollars' worth of commercial properties across the country. According to Aaron, on their first face-to-face meeting, John flew up to Buffalo on his private jet, with his chauffeur in tow, and rented a black Lincoln Town Car to shuttle him around. He met Aaron for lunch and got right to the point: "He asks, 'How much money are you looking for?' I'm like, 'I don't know, twenty million.' He goes, 'Son, my wife's got more money in her checking account than you've got in your whole goddamn fund.' I'm like, 'Okay, then write me a check.' He found that somewhat amusing, but not really." In the end, Aaron estimates that John gave him roughly $10 million.

Aaron subsequently flew down to Texas and gave reports, in person, on how the fund was performing. On his first trip, Aaron arrived by taxi at an office complex solely devoted to managing John's personal finances. "It looks like Versailles," he recalled. "I don't even know what you would call the architecture—I'm not an architecture buff. We pull up along this circular gravel driveway. You can imagine it, right? There are gardens and there's a guy with a fucking rifle there. Only in Texas, right? What do you need a guy with a rifle for? Because you can afford one. So you walk in and it is this beautiful marble palace. The doors open up, *whoosh*, and then there's a stairway that goes up to the top, and I'm waiting there after I talk to the receptionist, and he comes down the spiral staircase. He could've been like—what's-his-name from *Gone With the Wind*? Rhett Butler. All he needed was a girl with a gown on his arm made out of drapes.

"He walks me through the whole place. I get to look at every piece of art on the wall, which means nothing to me, and finally I go into the meeting room and they're all waiting." This is where Aaron was scheduled to give his report to a cadre of John's financial advisors. Aaron described some of the advisors as "really capable guys" and others simply as friends and family members. During his visits, "I'd give my presentation, and he'd berate me in front of everybody else. They all just sat there mutely. Clearly, they had seen this show before."

Even though John was the investor who had given Aaron the most money, he wasn't the one to whom Aaron felt the most indebted. There was another big investor, who had been instrumental in helping Aaron launch his fund. He was a Boston-based financier who began his career at Salomon Brothers and eventually founded his own hedge fund, which managed well over $1 billion in assets. The investor—who insisted that I identify him only by his middle name, Joseph—was a camera-shy man who religiously avoided the press.

Joseph had contributed roughly $1 million to Aaron's venture and had also helped him round up additional investors, back in 2008, when Aaron was just getting under way. "He was sort of like my godfather in this whole thing," said Aaron. "He introduced me to a lot of folks." Joseph found the idea of debt collections amusing, Aaron said, and relished Aaron's crackpot stories about the collectors, the debtors, and the craziness of the industry. "You got to understand, part of [the attraction] for him is the sheer joy of being able to tell people that he's involved in all these crazy things," said Aaron. "Just like a gambler who goes to a casino and says, 'I doubled down on black and won,' he likes to say, 'I'm involved in all these wild ventures that you, my friend, don't have the balls to do. But I do—and I make money.'"

Following the Great Recession and the $9 million Bank of America deal, however, it was unclear whether Joseph would make any money from his investment with Aaron. Aaron's fund was intended to exist for just four years, which meant that by the summer of 2012 the investors were supposed to be paid in full. But as that deadline came and went, Aaron was still collecting on some of the paper that he had purchased.

Many debtors, for example, had set up payment plans that involved giving Aaron fifty dollars a month for the next several years. Aaron could have sold these accounts prematurely—at a discount—but instead, he persuaded his investors that it was better to be patient and collect as much money as possible. The fund had, in effect, gone into extra innings and Aaron's investors had opted to sit, watch, and see how it all played out.

It was during this extended waiting period, in early 2013, that I accompanied Aaron on a trip to Boston for a meeting with Joseph. Joseph never expected Aaron to give him in-person updates; but Aaron was nonetheless determined to maintain a cordial relationship with him and, from time to time, meet in person.

We arranged to meet Joseph for dinner at Grill 23, an upscale restaurant a few blocks from Boston Common. The place was packed with the affluent, after-work crowd, mainly men in gray suits downing shots of bourbon and slicing into sixty-two-dollar Kobe cap steaks. Joseph was a middle-aged man with a paunch and florid complexion. He showed up in casual slacks and a blue short-sleeved shirt, complaining of how badly he had just golfed. With him were his college-age son and an old friend. The friend worked on Wall Street, for a Swiss bank, and he, too, asked that I identify him only by his middle name, Saul.

The maître d' led us upstairs to a table with four chairs. "I called and said it would be five of us," Aaron told the maître d'.

"Make it a table for six," Joseph interjected, as if he were annoyed. "He's not in charge," he said, gesturing toward Aaron. "I'm in charge." Then he turned to Aaron and said dismissively, "You can't set a table for five—you set it for six." Moments later, the waitress appeared to take our orders for drinks and appetizers. "Where is the crabmeat from?" asked Joseph. "Is it fresh or canned from the Philippines?"

"I'll find out, sir," she replied.

"What they do is they dig a hole in the ground and fill it with salt water, put in some crabs, feed them with fish guts, then send it all over the world in cans," Joseph said. "I don't want that." Moments later, the waitress returned and explained that the crabmeat was both fresh and domestic. Joseph nodded his head. That would do.

I soon asked Joseph about his hedge fund, but before he could answer, Saul intervened. "Joseph only succeeded because of when he was born," Saul said. He turned to his friend and said, "You had great timing, a big set of balls, and a force of personality." Joseph nodded his head appreciatively and went on to explain that, in the early 1990s, when he left his job on Wall Street, people thought he was crazy.

"This is the John Belushi of hedge funds," added Saul, pointing at his old friend.

Joseph waved off the analogy with a smile, noting that Belushi died in his thirties, whereas he was already in his fifties. He then joked: "I [recently] went to a strip club in New Orleans and I told my wife they have these clubs in Texas and Oklahoma and all over this country. They are not *all* supported by me. I don't have enough wealth."

"This is where rich men go and support single women with kids," Saul added thoughtfully. "Really, what better way to redistribute wealth?"

As drinks and appetizers arrived, Joseph began to recount his life story. He described growing up in a middle-class family with a father who earned a modest living in the lumber business. When I asked him if he always knew that he wanted to make money, he replied, "Absolutely. Always. It was just there. You asking that is like someone saying, 'Were you born gay?' People who want *this* have that spark from the beginning. It is *not* something you pick up sophomore year of college. Abso-fucking-lutely." The only question was how much money he could make. When running a hedge fund, he explained, there are no limits: "If you are an eye doctor, there are a limited number of procedures that you can do in a day. If you are a lawyer, there are a limited number of hours that you can bill. Every business has a cap. In this business, you can leverage O.P.M."—other people's money—"and make lots of money."

In addition to running his hedge fund, Joseph also enjoyed making a diverse range of investments with his own personal fortune. He had put his money into everything from restau-rants, to movies, to tanning salons, to Franklin Asset—which was Aaron's company. "If you are good at picking your invest-ments, you win more than you lose," he said. "It's like playing blackjack."

Aaron, looking for an entry point into the conversation, asked Joseph how his restaurant was faring. "It's like Franklin Asset," he replied dryly. "It's not out of business, but it's not making any money." There was an awkward silence and then Joseph continued. "If I have an investment, it is better for it to be either terminally ill or a home run. The worst is to have someone who is on life support. You can't kill him, and you can't party with him."

"I am in the life-support column," said Aaron.

Both Joseph and Saul were largely ignoring Aaron at this point. Perhaps this was because the two of them were very old friends. But there seemed to be another reason as well. Aaron, perhaps by no fault of his own, had underperformed—and Joseph was effectively telling him to shut up and listen because the right to pontificate about money, strippers, and life was a luxury that he hadn't earned. In a way, he was shaming Aaron for not being able to pay what he owed. It was, of course, the very tactic that Aaron's collectors sometimes used when they tried to embarrass debtors into paying what they owed.

When I pressed Joseph for details about his investments, he shook his head in frustration. "The mistake that people make is thinking about investments in absolute dollars," he told me. "You have to look at the whole picture. Most people do not know what they are worth because they don't think properly. If you asked ninety percent of people what their balance sheet looked like, they wouldn't know. People don't understand the bets that they are making." The key for him, he explained, was diversification. "That means that you only have one percent of your wealth invested in a company, so if it goes bust, you won't die." He estimated that he had invested just this, one percent of his wealth, with Aaron. Understanding this idea, he told me, was the key to making money.

"How much are you worth?" he asked me at one point.

"I don't know," I admitted to him. Then I added, rather sheepishly, "Well, I just bought a home, so I kind of know."

"You should know *exactly* what you are worth!" said Joseph, seeming genuinely disgusted with me. "You should know what your bets are."

I confessed that I was probably among the 90 percent of Americans who didn't know what their bets were—along with all of the debtors from Franklin Asset.

"Yes!" said Joseph. "The debtors from Franklin Asset, they don't know what their bets are. They are idiots. Like ninety percent of people, they don't know what they are worth. People make mistakes. But Franklin didn't put them in debt. They were just trying to collect. If the pitcher throws a bad pitch, and the hitter hits a home run, the batter isn't in the wrong. He is just doing his job." When it came to Franklin Asset, Joseph said that he simply saw an opportunity.

"It wasn't that I was so handsome and charming?" asked Aaron.

"No," said Joseph. "It was a window into an interesting world."

I was intrigued by the possibility that Joseph really wanted a "window" into this world—into the lives of the people whose debts he owned. I thought for a moment of Joanna, returning to her modest apartment in the suburbs, after working a sixteen-hour shift at the assisted-living facility, doing a final load of laundry before she went to bed. It seemed strange to think that I was staring across the table at the man who had purchased her debt for a few pennies on the dollar.

But apparently that wasn't the sort of window that Joseph wanted to look through. When I asked him if he ever paused to consider the lives of the people whose debts he owned, he said no. "Let me explain it this way. A guy came to me with a business plan to open stores with tanning booths. He wanted seventy-five thousand dollars. You turn the tanning lights on and the girls come. I think it's a shitty business. It's carcinogenic. I wouldn't let my family do it. But the numbers are compelling. And I got all my money back in six months. The beds were paid for. We have five thousand women who are signed up to pay for the annual fee. It's not illegal and it throws off cash. So, if someone is going to collect on people's debts, I might as well be in bed with them, if I can make a profit. It turns out that the suntanning business is better than the debt-collecting business."

"So where do you draw the line?" I asked. "Is it simply a matter of legality?"

Joseph ducked the question and instead replied, "We own a bar, we can go there later, and they decided, as a policy, to stay open until two a.m. Now in the city of Boston, the subway, what's it called . . ."

"The T," answered Joseph's son.

"Yes, the T," said Joseph, nodding appreciatively. "I have never been on it, so I don't give a fuck, but it often shuts down at twelve twenty-five a.m. We decided to stay open to two a.m. because we know the crowd will come in late, like after a Red Sox game, and there aren't many other places to go. Now there is a risk running your business like that, because if someone gets drunk, drives home, and gets in an accident, they may sue. But I am just a limited partner." Because of this, explained Joseph, he was not legally liable.

Again, I pressed him on where he would draw the line on what he would invest in. *Was it just a matter of legal liability?*

"Prostitution is legal in Kings Cross in Sydney, Australia," replied Joseph, still dancing around my question. "You can legally own and operate a whorehouse there. I have a friend who bought one. He made a lot of money there. Now I would *not* buy a fucking whorehouse because of my wife and our domestic bliss. So there is a line—and it's not just legality."

As dinner drew to a close, a waiter brought over a folder with the bill. It was roughly $600 for the five of us. Joseph didn't touch it. Saul went for his wallet, as if to pay. "Let them pay," said Joseph. "He has been pumping me for information," he said, gesturing at me. "And he owes me," he added, pointing at Aaron.

When I first met Aaron, in Buffalo, my impression was that he was the rust belt's equivalent of landed gentry. I thought of him much the way I thought of William Weld, the former governor of Massachusetts, who, when asked how he had made his money, famously replied, "The Welds don't make money. They have money." I might have thought this way because I myself had grown up in Buffalo and knew the aura of wealth and glamour that surrounded the Siegel family. Aaron came from a different world than I did. I had gone to public school and had a decidedly more modest childhood, and perhaps for this reason I was somewhat impressed by his mansion on Soldiers Place and the ease with which he breezed through the doors at the Buffalo Club. By the standards of Buffalo, Aaron was a veritable plutocrat. But it was clear to me now that within the context of this industry, Aaron was a beleaguered middleman. The debtors owed Brandon, Brandon owed Aaron, and Aaron owed his investors. To make matters worse, or at least more stressful, Aaron was sandwiched between two larger-than-life alpha males: Joseph and Brandon.

When I mentioned this idea to Aaron, he embraced the notion that Joseph and Brandon were quite similar. "You're totally on track," he told me. "Clearly they are doppelgangers." One of them was Superman, he suggested, and the other was Superman's slightly twisted alter ego, Bizarro: "Both have a tremendous amount of bluster, both have experienced a great degree of success, and both live high on the hog." And they both—especially Joseph—don't "really give a fuck about you." Almost immediately after saying this, Aaron corrected himself, asserting that, at the end of the day, Brandon did care. "His heart's in the right place," said Aaron, "but that doesn't mean he won't fuck you over."

Aaron's principal concern with Brandon was getting every dollar that Brandon owed him. According to Aaron's deputy, Lilly, this was a real problem. She says that Brandon was often "very broke" and that he would sometimes erupt at her, "screaming and yelling." Aaron eventually decided that the best way to get his money would be to have his own company, Franklin Asset, process the payments that debtors made to Brandon's collectors. This way, Brandon never actually had his hands on the money. Aaron sent Lilly up to Maine to review Brandon's bookkeeping and inaugurate the new system. Lilly subsequently called Aaron on the phone, in tears, alleging that Brandon was drinking whiskey and suggesting that they go to a casino. In the end, Lilly says that she implemented the new payment system, but not without considerable heartache.

"I was begging Aaron to discontinue the relationship with Brandon," Lilly told me. Aaron, however, clung to his conviction that he had a strong personal relationship with Brandon and that Brandon would ultimately always come through for him. For her part, Lilly speculated that Aaron stuck with Brandon because his collectors were good, his agency generated numbers that he needed to keep investors happy, and Brandon had a network of clients who were willing to buy older debt once Franklin Asset was done with it. Plus, Lilly said, Aaron was "charmed" by Brandon's tough-guy persona. "[Aaron's] popular with the ladies, but he's not very popular with, well . . . he rubs a lot of people the wrong way." According to Lilly, Aaron liked "to have an ally in Brandon, who is loud and who could fight his battles."

Even after Lilly made her trip to Maine and implemented the new credit-card processing system, Brandon continued to owe Aaron money from various other deals that they made together. Around the time that we met Joseph for dinner, in early 2013, Aaron claimed that Brandon owed him roughly $30,000. He had been calling Brandon regularly, reminding him to pay up. The irony of the situation wasn't lost on Aaron. He had become a debt buyer so he wouldn't have to hound surly debtors into paying their bills, and now he was hounding a former armed robber instead.

As it turns out, Brandon was facing some rather serious challenges of his own. Part of the problem was that the federal government had finally begun cracking down on banks and debt buyers. In 2010, Congress passed the Dodd-Frank Wall Street Reform and Consumer Protection Act. The stated aim of the act was "to promote the financial stability of the United States by improving accountability and transparency in the financial system," put an end to bailouts paid by the American taxpayers, and "protect consumers from abusive financial services practices." The Dodd-Frank Act also paved the way for the creation of the Consumer Financial Protection Bureau (CFPB) in 2011. The idea for the CFPB actually dated back to 2007, when Elizabeth Warren—then a professor at Harvard Law School—first suggested the idea, arguing that middle-class Americans needed to be better protected from the many financial institutions that preyed upon them. By early 2012, the CFPB was very much a reality, and its new acting director—Richard Cordray—announced that it would start "supervising" some of the nation's larger debt collectors in order to "help restore confidence that the federal government is standing beside the American consumer." This reform, which consumer advocates and champions of the poor had pushed mightily for, would—perhaps inevitably—adversely affect the Aarons and Brandons of the world.

Rumors soon began to circulate in the debt-buying industry that the banks—fearful of their new regulators—would soon become more cautious about whom they sold paper to. In the summer of 2012, I was visiting the office of a veteran debt broker named Tom Borges, and I listened in on a conversation that he had with a high-ranking member of DBA International, a leading association of debt buyers. In that call, the DBA official speculated that the banks might prohibit the "resale" of credit-card debt altogether; in other words, the banks would sell it once—to a reputable buyer—but not allow the buyer ever to sell that debt again. This wasn't even the full extent of it. By 2012, Chase—the nation's largest bank—had already suspended the sale of *all* credit-card debt. The bank didn't admit this publicly, and never has, but a spokesman for Chase told me the suspension had been in effect at least since late 2011. This was almost certainly due to the special scrutiny that Chase was receiving from federal regulators.

In any case, none of this boded well for debt brokers such as Tom. He concluded that he would have to evolve and find new types of paper—such as debt resulting from cosmetic surgery—that didn't have such restrictions. "I am going to have to reinvent myself," said Tom.

Debt buyers faced another problem as well, namely that the banks had become much choosier about whom they would lend money to in the first place. Those people who did get loans typically had good credit scores and were likely to repay what they borrowed. That meant fewer debts were being charged off, sold for pennies on the dollar, and winding up in the hands of buyers like Brandon. Brandon himself was somewhat insulated from this. His specialty was older debt—"crap," as he put it—and there was still plenty of that on the market and would be for some time. But the shortage of newer paper would, inevitably, drive up the cost of older paper. The bottom line was that the supply of paper was, at least for the time being, diminishing. A drought was coming and no one would be totally immune to it. All of these factors were starting to make Brandon's job harder and less profitable. Brandon was struggling—not just to make money, but to see a way forward for the collection agency and brokerage firm that he owned and operated in Bangor, Maine.

I was eager to see Brandon's operation in Maine for several reasons. I wanted to see how his collectors handled the likes of Joanna, Theresa, and the other debtors from the Package whose accounts had passed through his offices. But I also wanted to see how Brandon was planning to survive the imminent drought. Somehow or another, Brandon had to find a way to exploit new inefficiencies in the paper market. He would have to reinvent himself or he would simply have to get that much better at finding deals and acquiring diamonds in the rough, like the Package. His own survival depended on it. In fact, as I would soon see for myself, the survival of an entire clan of Brandon's friends and family was depending on it.

6

BRANDON'S PEOPLE

Brandon's agency was situated right in the heart of downtown Bangor, in between a dingy-looking school for dancers and a curio store whose billboard featured an old sea captain and advertised gold coins, costume jewelry, and "small antiques." The agency occupied a stately old brick building from 1911 that had once operated as a hotel. The first floor housed the actual agency and the higher floors served as a flophouse where Brandon's collectors were allowed to sleep, eat, and shower for fifty dollars a week. Brandon had chosen to base himself in Maine because regulators in his native state of Massachusetts had apparently made it difficult for former felons to obtain licenses to run their own collection agencies. "They have been trying to stop me from working in this business for years because I did ten years in the can and I am a three-time loser," Brandon explained to me. The authorities in Maine had proved more hospitable.

I visited Brandon several times in 2012 and 2013. On my first visit I found him strutting up and down the main hallway, puffing out his chest and speaking in his preternaturally loud voice. He was exhorting his collectors to hook a few last "payers" before the business day ended. "Fifteen minutes!" he yelled. "We need a buzzer beater. We need a good one!" His collectors, who seemed to range in number from five to fifteen depending on the day, tucked into their respective cubicles, trying desperately to maintain a semblance of decorum and muffle the shouts of the madman who was their boss.

One of Brandon's employees spoke up. He was Jeremy Mountain, the tall, fair-haired, earnest-looking kid in his late twenties who had accompanied Brandon down to Buffalo and confronted Bill at his corner store. Jeremy started to say something—a question, an objection, an excuse-me-your-fly-is-open—but he never got it out: Brandon pointed to a sign on the wall that read, NO WHINING, CRYING, BITCHING, MOANING, COMPLAINING, BLUBBERING, OR OTHERWISE EXPRESSING INVALID OPINIONS. Jeremy looked at me with faux-wounded eyes and said, "This is how I am treated for all my service to this office."

Jeremy, the son of a paper mill worker, had dropped out of college, started working for Brandon as a collector, and now headed sales and compliance for the agency. He told me that he'd quit his job six times because of Brandon's chaotic management style, which included moving Jeremy's desk no fewer than fifty times in four years. "He's never satisfied. He always wants to do better, better, better," lamented Jeremy. "He's always [saying], 'Complacency kills.'" Complaints aside, Jeremy revered his boss, noting that he had treated him like a son. "He's just a genius—probably not when you're talking about molecular science geniuses, but socially and businesswise, the guy is as smart as they come."

Jeremy and the other employees in the office seemed to take a perverse pride in what a hard-ass their boss was. "We had this guy working here, who was a former marine, and he had done like three or four years in Iraq," explained Jeremy. "He quit here after one month—he said it was the most hostile work environment he had ever been in." The other collectors in the office loved this story, just as they loved their boss's reputation as a former bank robber. The collectors were mainly native Mainers, including several from the more rural parts of the state. In these regions, one collector told me, you often didn't know whether it was your "daddy" or your "uncle" who sired you and so you simply called all of the potential candidates "duncle."

Brandon's collectors saw their boss as the great redeemer. One of them, who struck me as especially earnest, told me that he was one of the "good eggs" at the office, despite being a felon. "I had a drug habit, and the only way to support a drug habit is to deal. No one would hire me because of my record except Brandon. We *here* are people who have done really stupid stuff, but we are intelligent, and Brandon has no trouble redeeming us." Another collector, named Jason Robinson, admitted to me, rather sheepishly, that he had gone to jail for accidentally shooting off his gun. He had been on a city bus, en route to sell a .357 Magnum to a friend of his, when he fell asleep. He claims to have had too much Xanax. Shortly thereafter, the .357 Magnum went off and the bullet tore a hole in the side of the bus. When the young man got out of jail, Brandon gave him a job as a collector. For a while, Jason lived upstairs in what used to be an old hotel room. Jason said that the floor he inhabited was nice enough, but that the building's upper levels were abandoned and creepy, furnished with claw-foot bathtubs and antiquated heating stoves. "Homeless people used to climb in the back window upstairs and sleep up there," he said.

For his part, Brandon thrived on the notion that he was the great father figure to his band of former miscreants. "I'll always give people a shot," he told me. In fact, as a matter of company policy, the only people that he wouldn't hire were "rats" and "child molesters." He added, almost apologetically, "I gotta draw the line somewhere."

In addition to all the locals whom he hired, Brandon also had quite a few of his family members working for him—his mother, nephews, and grown children. I met one such relative, a guy named Tony, who lived with Brandon but nonetheless was uncertain how exactly he was related to him. A collector named Brent offered to clarify matters.

"Tony is Brandon's brother or his nephew, depending on how you tell it, though he is actually his cousin," explained Brent.

"Brandon's mother is my great-aunt," added Tony helpfully.

"So he is your second cousin?" asked Brent.

"We make no distinction in our family," replied Tony.

Brent finally concluded, with a chortle, that Brandon was probably a kind of a "duncle" to Tony.

For a small shop, Brandon insisted the key to survival was "the lost art of skip tracing." Skip tracing is industry slang for sleuthing and tracking debtors down—finding out where they work, where they live, and who their neighbors are. Bigger agencies often used computer software to "batch skip," generating leads through an automated system that searched through a variety of online databases. Such a system could be profitable, explained Brandon, but it was also inefficient and allowed a lot of debtors to slip through the cracks. At a smaller shop like his, with just a few dozen collectors, they could pick through a file and identify the debtors who had been missed by the "batch skip," and then, with a little legwork, collect on their debts.

According to the Brandon Wilson school of skip tracing, you started by identifying and then calling the neighbor. Legally, under the provisions of the Fair Debt Collection Practices Act, a collector is allowed to call a neighbor only to verify a debtor's contact information such as phone number or home address; and a collector may not mention anything about a debt or ask the neighbor to relay a message. "But if the neighbor volunteers to pass along a message, you can say: 'Gee, do you think you can leave my name and number on the mailbox?'" insisted Brandon. In such a scenario, Brandon wouldn't say he was a debt collector. The trick was simply prompting the neighbor to help out. "I will say things like: 'They don't have my number—and I am calling all the way from Bangor, Maine—I don't know what I am going to do.' When the debtor gets the message, nine times out of ten they will call us, even if just to say, 'Fuck you—don't call my neighbor again.' And that's what we want. We want that chance to get them on the phone and turn them. I can say, 'Look, man, you can rant and rave all you want, but if you cleared this up we wouldn't have to call your neighbor. Let's clear this thing up.' And you just try to talk him down." Apparently, the very best person to contact was a debtor's scornful ex-spouse: "They'll tell you, 'Here is his number, here is his mother's number, here is his slutty girlfriend's number . . .' We will usually put it on mute and say, 'We got a rat—we got a rat!'"

After debtors were located, and then contacted, the next step was to classify them appropriately. To this end, Brandon had developed his own quasi-scientific taxonomy, placing debtors into some thirty-eight different species or types. If a debtor hung up, he was a "DHU"; if he procrastinated, he was a "Stall"; if he bothered to call back, but did nothing else, he was a "Call Back"; if he bounced a check, he was a "Bounce"; if he promised a payment arrangement, he was a "PPA"; if he broke that pledge, he was "Broken Promise"; if he started to make payments, but then stopped or broke the deal, he was a "Broken Payment"; if he was very ill, he was a "Health"; and if, for some reason, he ended up in prison, he was simply a "Jail." Each of these types had their own value. For example, a DHU was a sorry specimen because he had hung up and likely would do so again; a CB was a better prospect, because he had at least bothered to call back; a PPA had potential, because he made a promise to pay and thus acknowledged the debt was his; a Broken Promise had failed to honor his guarantee, but that wasn't entirely bad, because you could now use that against him; and a Broken Payment simply needed a little nudging because he had started to pay and just needed to get back on track.

Using a software system that Brandon himself had developed, he could program the office's auto-dialer to call only certain debtors whom he had classified. One day, I watched as the auto-dialer called Broken Promises, Broken Payments, Bounces, and Call Backs. The system was configured so that as soon as the debtor picked up, the call was routed to a collector. Brandon sat at his desk quietly, listening as his collectors worked the phones. Sitting nearby was Jason, the collector who had gone to jail for accidentally shooting his gun on a public bus. Jason was on the phone with an elderly debtor named Patsy who was a Stall. Brandon shook his head irritably, saying he didn't like how "snotty" Jason was being with her. He then walked over to Jason's desk, took the phone from him, and introduced himself to Patsy, explaining that he was the office manager.

"I'd love to tell you to forget the whole thing, Patsy," said Brandon. "I have a mother, I have a grandmother, but I can't do that. Unfortunately, it's in your name, it's under your social, and the balance is due. I could give you a settlement, I could work out some kind of hardship plan with you."

"Sir," said Patsy. "I get social security and that's it."

"Right," said Brandon.

"I barely get enough to live on," added Patsy.

"Right, well, I understand times are hard, ma'am," said Brandon. "There are a lot of people in that situation."

Patsy then claimed that she did not recognize the loan, which—according to Brandon's computer records—originated from "Republic Bank & Trust." "I've never had anything to do with the Republic Bank," said Patsy. After reviewing the information on Jason's computer screen, Brandon himself wasn't certain what type of loan this was. "Unfortunately, ma'am, this could be a payday loan for all I know, but I don't have an option where I can tell you to forget the whole thing."

"Sir, I can't do anything," said Patsy. "I have ten dollars to my name. Well, I'm sorry. There's nothing I can do." Then she hung up—a move that, ostensibly, transformed her from a Stall to a DHU—which, needless to say, was a downgrade from Brandon's perspective.

Despite countless exchanges like this one, which proved ultimately fruitless, it was Brandon's belief—as a matter of practicality—that it made sense to be civil to debtors. "Most people want to pay their bills," he said. "If you talk to them like a normal human being, it works. It is a big misconception that people don't want to pay. When the debtors do the screaming, and the ducking out, and the complaining, it's just them lashing out because they can't pay. The public thinks no one wants to pay. But the truth is, people lash out when they can't pay. If you called people up and they had ten grand in the bank, they would pay instantly."

Most of Brandon's collectors appeared to be won over by the merits of this argument. They strove for empathy—trying to "marry the debtor," as one of them put it—simply because it was lucrative. Brandon was a master at this. One day, I listened in while he tried to collect on an old, unpaid cell-phone bill with a face value of $401. "I'm gonna need a call back no later than Friday at five p.m. Eastern Standard Time, if you have any intentions at all of handling this thing voluntarily," he told the debtor. Brandon went on to say that, if the man didn't pay by the end of the month, there would be added fees and costs and the bill might be much higher. "So by all means, verify it [the bill], but I need to set up a payment arrangement to clear up your good name."

"Yeah, well, I'll get my lawyer involved," replied the debtor.

"If you want to get a lawyer involved about a three-hundred-dollar bill . . ."

"No, no, no," said the debtor. "You don't understand."

"You go ahead, sir," said Brandon patiently.

The debtor went on to claim that he was the victim of identity fraud and he suspected that his ex-wife was running up bills in his name.

"You know, that happens a lot," said Brandon sympathetically. "Hey, and if you want to contact your ex and tell her that you found another fraud that she did, and tell her to pay us [the money] before you go and make a report of identity theft to the police, that'd be fine." He added quickly, however, that ultimately this bill was in *his* name. "I'm trying to help your credit," said Brandon. "Whether she did it or not, it's affecting you."

"Hey, man, I ended up in the hospital for six months," replied the debtor. "I got shot. She shot my ass all over. So it ain't no big deal, I understand."

"She ain't no good, huh?" said Brandon.

"Oh, she's a drug dealer," said the debtor. "Drug lord. I got involved with the wrong woman." He added that he had even "ended up in jail because of her."

Brandon seemed genuinely fascinated by the possibility that the man's ex was a "drug lord" and, at one point in the conversation, he asked what kind of drugs she was caught selling.

"Ice," replied the debtor.

"Ice," said Brandon. "A lot of ice or petty ice jobs?"

"Five keys [kilos]."

"Five keys of ice," said Brandon, impressed. "Do you have any police reports saying that she perpetrated fraud against you in the past?"

The debtor said that he wanted to check with his lawyer about this.

And then Brandon again began making his pitch. "In a perfect world, what could I do for you?" he asked.

"In a perfect world there's nothing I can do, man—no perfect way out of here," replied the debtor. The debtor then suggested that he would talk with his lawyer and call Brandon back. Brandon ignored the suggestion and, instead, asked the man about his time in jail. "There might be special programs that I can do as far as helping you out," said Brandon. "When did you go to prison?"

"I was stuck in county for her," said the debtor.

Brandon asked a few more probing questions, then he

remarked, ever so casually, "Well, you know what, if you can prove that you have some kind of ulterior struggles, I might be able to get this settlement down to one hundred twenty bucks or maybe even a ten-dollars-a-month hardship plan."

In the end, Brandon was unable to persuade the man to make a payment, but he had come close—in no small part because he had successfully "married" the debtor and then offered him a "special" deal based on the debtor's unique life circumstances. It was an impressive "talk-off," as they call it in the business.

Some of Brandon's collectors shared his gift, a mix of volubility, pathos, and cunning; others, however, seemed helplessly clumsy or standoffish on the phones. On one of my visits, the collectors were ribbing a guy named Zach, a former welder, who had the distinction of being the month's worst collector. "I sound like a snarky dickhead on the phone," Zach admitted to me glumly, as if he were describing a congenital condition. "It's just something about the way I speak that elicits a very negative reaction in most people."

As the day wore on, several of Brandon's collectors began clamoring for me to get on the phones and try collecting a debt. I resisted, both because I preferred to watch from afar and—quite honestly—I wasn't too enthused about the prospect of hounding poor people over the telephone. "It's the only way you'll really understand what it's like," one of them told me. "We will give you a pseudonym, like Mark Twain," said Brandon. "Everybody here starts as Teddy Green. The real Teddy Green was a Bruins player from the seventies." Reluctantly, I agreed.

After assenting to a confidentiality agreement—saying I would not disclose the full names, social security numbers, addresses, or account numbers of any debtors—I began training with Jason and then got to work. I sat down at a computer, put on a headset, and logged on to the computer system. Instantly, the auto-dialer was sending calls my way. There was a beep, a detailed electronic record would flash onto my computer screen, and then I'd hear a debtor saying, "Hello?" On one of my first calls, I connected with a woman who owed several hundred dollars on an old cell-phone bill.

"I'm calling because I'm trying to follow up on a loan that we had on record for you guys and I'm wondering whether there's any way we can set up a payment plan for you," I told her. As soon as I said this, I cringed. I knew instinctively that this opening gambit was weak. I wouldn't pay me, if I were the debtor. I tried to recover: "The balance was at 1,441 dollars, which I know is a lot, there's a bunch of fees and interest, but we're able to . . ." At this point, Brandon, who was listening to me, whispered, "Nine hundred dollars." "Offer you a settlement of nine hundred bucks, which is about five hundred less than the balance."

"I'm not working right now," the debtor told me.

I asked her how long she had been unemployed, working hard to keep my tone measured and sympathetic, doing my best to "marry her"—a notion that now seemed rather absurd. "We talk to a lot of folks who are in kind of a similar spot," I told her. "One thing that we can work out is a hardship payment plan, where it's just fifty dollars a month." At one point, the woman told me that she could probably pay me on the fifteenth of the month, but mentioned that she didn't have a credit card to make the payment. We spoke for a few more minutes until, rather abruptly, she hung up on me.

Brandon, who was standing directly behind me—and seemed to be enjoying his role as my coach—immediately commenced with the postgame commentary. "You should have given her our address and made her promise to send the check on the fifteenth," he said, shaking his head. "Then, when she didn't pay, she would be a Broken Promise. When you call her back, you say: 'You promised to pay and you didn't.' Then you're *not* talking about *if* they owe the money, you're talking about her making good on what she promised." My mistake wasn't in failing to collect, it was that I had failed to upgrade her to a better class of debtor.

Moments later the phone ran again and I was speaking with another woman, who owed a balance of several thousand dollars on her credit card. I suggested that we work out a payment plan. "I'm not going to be able to do any of this," she told me. "I was just answering out of, uh, what would you call it? You know, good manners."

"I really appreciate it," I told her.

"I'm not a deadbeat—it kind of sounds like I am—but I just got ill, and that was a long time ago, and I'm barely staying afloat. You know, the more I can do for myself and not cost the state money[, the better]. That's where I'm at." I asked her what kind of illness she had. She explained that she was bipolar. "It changed my entire situation and my life, I mean the financial part," she explained. "I wasn't able to pay bills and then I had no credit." She told me that she had managed her condition "pretty well," but added, "I know that I'm getting close to losing it, which would mean going to a hospital and, you know, a recovery period." As she spoke, her voice sounded shaky. I wanted to hang up the phone, but I forced myself to press on.

"Is there any way that you could even set up even a modest payment to help pay this off?" I asked.

"No, no," said the woman. "Are you not hearing me?" Then she hung up.

I looked back sheepishly at Brandon, who was still standing directly behind me.

"You know what you should have said?" he asked.

I shrugged.

"You should have said: 'I understand that these are tough times, and you have been through some hardships, but I got ninety-year-old ladies on oxygen who are sending twenty-five dollars a month, as a show of good faith, so certainly there is something you can do to start paying off this debt.'"

I nodded my head, sighed, and looked up at the clock. There were still a few minutes left before all of the collectors in the office got a fifteen-minute cigarette break, and—as far as I was concerned—that break couldn't come soon enough. I was a terrible collector. There was no doubt about it. I lacked Brandon's easy rapport with the debtors and his innate sense of when to segue from courtship back to the unpleasant matter of collecting. Most of all, I lacked something more fundamental, something more visceral: I lacked the drive and the hunger to make my commission. But this, I realized, was largely a matter of life circumstances. I was a comfortable upper-middle-class guy with a house, two cars, and a wife who was a doctor. I knew that if circumstances were different, if I were poorer and worried about my family—like so many debt collectors—then somehow or another I would find a way to collect.

Brandon wasn't kidding when he told me that he employed virtually every single person in his family. One day in Maine, I wandered into the basement and encountered an elderly woman making cheesesteak sandwiches on an electric griddle. This was Darlene, the agency's official cook and Brandon's mother. "You can call me Ma Barker," she told me, in a heavy Boston accent. She wore jeans and a T-shirt.

"Why Ma Barker?" I asked.

"Ma Barker was this woman in the 1920s who had her sons rob banks for her—but then she kept all the money," she said with a laugh. "Truth is, I always tried to keep my boys out of trouble, but it never worked."

Brandon eventually joined our conversation and told me that, despite everything he had gone through—all the arrests, lockups, and hardships—he never doubted his own self-worth, in part (surprisingly enough) because of his lineage. "I am related to John Quincy Adams," he told me. Brandon has traced his Irish lineage back to his great-grandfather, a vaudeville actor from Cork whose name—oddly enough—was Major English.

Darlene, who was still sitting nearby, chimed in: "We are also related to John Thompson of Thompson Island in Boston Harbor."

"That is why we have some Indian blood," Brandon said.

"Thompson or some other relative was kidnapped in the war of 1812 or the French and Indian War," Darlene explained, "and he brought back a squaw. And that is where the Indian blood came from."

"Who knows *who* was fucking *who* back in the toolsheds in the 1800s," added Brandon. "They can write whatever they want on paper."

Family lineage only did so much, Brandon concluded. After that it was his common sense—and his street sense—that enabled him to survive.

"I learned all my kicks and punches in dancing school," he told us.

"Dancing school?" I said incredulously. "You?"

"He wasn't afraid to try things," said Darlene.

"I went to the school, and for the recital we did the 'Kung Fu Fighting' song. You remember that one?"

"He had a lot of confidence. He wasn't afraid of dancing."

"Years later, I used those moves to beat people up."

"That's not why I sent him to dancing school."

"It was three gay ten-year-olds, me, and a bunch of chicks."

"They were all there to control their weight," said Darlene.

"That was a long time ago."

"I used to worry about you."

"Do you still worry, Ma?"

"I have two dead kids. You could die of a heart attack any day because you eat too much bacon. You can't call life. Life calls you."

"Do you ever feel bad for what you put your mom through?" I asked.

"Yeah," said Brandon. "But I feel bad for what life put me through. This collections gig has been my salvation. When I was younger someone told me, 'Put on a suit and you can rob anybody.' Truth is, I haven't changed much, but many people respect me now, because I have a business and property and look respectable. Now that I have these trappings, they treat me with respect. If you can pay the right lawyer or have the right look, you are respectable. If you walk in with a ripped shirt and a public defender, you are an animal."

Respectable or not, Brandon's shop generated complaints. Just a week before my initial visit, a debtor told the Better Business Bureau that one of Brandon's collectors had threatened to inform his employer about his debt and then taunted him, saying, "When are you going to step up and start being a man about this?" There was another complaint, filed that same week, from a debtor who claimed that another of Brandon's collectors had been "calling family members of mine and hinting that I would be in serious legal trouble if this bill wasn't paid off." In both cases, Brandon's agency wrote a reply explaining, "we take all complaints seriously" and "we have closed the account based on your complaint." In both instances, the Better Business Bureau noted that the disputes appeared to have been resolved.

Of these two complaints, the one involving the threat of a lawsuit was the more serious because the Fair Debt Collection Practices Act prohibits nonlawyers from making such threats. According to Aaron's deputy, Lilly, a number of Brandon's collectors had made such threats in the past. The collectors used a "legal talk-off," said Lilly, which falsely led debtors to believe that they might end up in court—or worse—if they didn't pay up. Aaron tolerated this behavior, said Lilly, because Brandon's collectors were so effective in collecting on his paper. Aaron disputes this, maintaining that he was sued on only a few occasions because of conduct at Brandon's agency—which is inevitable—and that he wouldn't have tolerated more suits simply because it would have been too costly.

On one occasion, I overheard one of Brandon's collectors tell a debtor to pay up or risk facing a "summons"—a not-so-subtle hint. Making a threat like this was a calculated risk. It could help you collect, or it could get you sued. Brandon once paid $16,000 in damages, for example, to a debtor after one of his collectors threatened to sue. After that, Brandon strongly discouraged this talk-off or any like it.

Another consumer also filed a complaint with the Better Business Bureau, saying that Brandon's agency was trying to collect a debt that was beyond the statute of limitations in the consumer's home state of Pennsylvania. Of course, Brandon prided himself on his skill at collecting on older paper—"out-of-stat" debt—that debtors could no longer be sued over. Brandon favored taking a direct approach, reminding debtors that they were still "morally" obligated to pay. Interestingly, once a debtor makes a payment on an out-of-stat debt—no matter

how small—this transaction often resets the statute of limitations. It effectively revives the debt, bringing it back to life.
And so some collectors do whatever they can to exhort, cajole,
browbeat, or even deceive consumers into reviving a debt. The
FTC has recommended that states require collectors to warn
debtors about this trick. But this is ultimately a matter that has
been left to the states, and the vast majority of them have not
yet acted on this suggestion. In any case, Brandon's agency
responded to the complaint from Pennsylvania by stating, "We
understand that it may be frustrating to receive a call on an
older account, but there are no laws that prevent [us from] attempting to collect on an account past the statute of limitation,
ONLY in litigating or implying further civil action." And, as far
as the law is concerned, this was completely right.

Brandon transitioned from collecting on debt to buying and
selling it with well-practiced ease. At one point, I was chatting
with Brandon when we were interrupted by Jeremy Mountain,
who told us that there was an important call that he needed to
take. The guy on the phone wanted to sell him a portfolio of
credit-card debt, most of which had been charged off in 2002
and was out-of-stat.

"You want to see me make fifty thousand dollars?" asked
Brandon.

I nodded.

"This is a piece of paper I am going to buy for one hundred
thousand and flip for one hundred fifty thousand tomorrow,"
he said. The face value of the file—the total amount of dollars
owed on all the accounts—was $100 million, meaning that
Brandon would be buying this file for one tenth of a penny
per dollar. Brandon grabbed the phone. "I will give you one

hundred," he said into the receiver. "It is pretty beat up. You got a couple of huge balances on top. I don't know what I can get for it. There is twenty million on top that I don't even want. If you pulled it out, I would still take it. Let's get something done. Get back to me."

As it turns out, Brandon already had the buyer lined up. "The buyer thinks he's getting a deal," explained Brandon. "He thinks it's worth three hundred thousand because he put it through his computerized scoring model, and based on the dates, states where the creditors live, and agencies that worked it previously, he thinks he knows exactly how much he can liquidate."

"Is he right?

Brandon gave me a look, as if to say, *Maybe.*

"They got their sophisticated scoring models, I got my eyeball," Brandon said.

"Will the seller give you this file for one hundred thousand?" I asked.

Brandon nodded and explained that the broker, who was helping the seller arrange the deal, was a friend of Brandon's and had told him that he could push the seller down to $100,000. Brandon lived on tips like this. "Insider trading is alive and well in the debt business," he told me.

Brandon got back on the phone and called the prospective buyer. The buyer understood, implicitly, that Brandon was acting as a middleman and that Brandon had not yet even purchased this piece of debt. The buyer also knew, however, that Brandon was vetting this file for him and giving him his word that the file was legitimate. "If there is any problem, if anyone tries to burn us, it is *not* on you, it is on me," Brandon told the buyer. "If that happens, I am in the car going to his place and I smash the guy's fucking head in. You know that." The buyer was appeased and, shortly after this, the deal went through.

Brandon was always on the prowl for would-be partners with deep pockets—or even not-so-deep pockets—who could help fund deals that he lined up. One night I went out for a drink with Brandon, and we ended up bumping into one such partner, a handsome young man in his mid-twenties from Thailand named Ahm Kongsuriya. Ahm had a slim, athletic build and wore jeans, a white T-shirt, and a black baseball cap emblazoned with red sequins. Ahm owned a sushi restaurant in Bangor, and sometimes when he had cash to spare, he invested his money with Brandon. "He usually gets me a fifty-percent return over the course of six months," said Ahm, who seemed very pleased. "I don't need any contract with him."

"That's right," said Brandon, as he put his arm around Ahm. "My word is my bond."

As the night went on, many of the people who entered the bar—mainly twenty-somethings dressed like Brooklyn hipsters—seemed to recognize Brandon. At one point, Brandon peeled out a thick wad of hundreds, which he had won at the casino the night before, and bought everyone a round of drinks. Soon after that, a guy in his early twenties, with an immaculately trimmed beard, approached us and introduced himself. He said his name was Kristopher Snyder and that he was studying to be a nurse practitioner. Then he turned to Brandon: "You're the guy who beat up the Nazi, aren't you?"

Brandon nodded.

Kristopher recounted a story from a night not long before, when a very large man with a swastika tattooed on his throat had showed up at this bar and started heckling people—one of them being Quincy, Brandon's chauffeur, who was African-American. As Kristopher told it, Brandon, despite being much older and smaller than the Nazi, dragged the Nazi out of the bar and beat him savagely. "The Nazi was way out of line—every step of the way that evening," Kristopher said. "He had it coming."

"I took it to that Nazi," confirmed Brandon proudly. "I am a perfect gentleman. But that Nazi was going to get banged out for that tattoo and that Nazi nonsense. I was just waiting for him to disrespect anyone."

"I think he sensed that," Kristopher said.

"I warned him twice."

"You went animalistic on him."

Brandon nodded and returned to the bar for another drink. Kristopher eyed him as he walked away. "He is the kind of guy who knows what he wants, and if he can't get it psychologically, he will get it physically," he said. "He is like a pit bull, dude."

Late that evening, after Brandon and I both had had more to drink than we should have, we sat together on a street bench under the canopy of an old tree. It was a temperate night, and cool air rustled through the branches overhead. "I thought that once I had enough money, happiness would follow," Brandon told me with uncharacteristic somberness. "It's not true. I am a worse person with money. The more money I have, the more I am like Thurston Howell, and the less I have, the more I am like Robin Hood."

"So why do you do it?" I asked.

Brandon shrugged. He then told me the story about the day, back in late 2008, when he had brokered Aaron's $9 million purchase of Bank of America paper—the "senior citizen" debt, as Aaron put it. "I made a four-hundred-ninety-seven-thousand-dollar commission for brokering that deal with Aaron," he told me. "I made the deal at eleven a.m., and at one a.m. that night I was still in the office working. I called my friend and said, 'Bring me some cigarettes; I am still at the office.' He got there and said, 'You made half a million dollars this morning. What the fuck are you still doing at the office?' I thought it was all about money until I had it—and then I realized it was just about outdoing the next guy."

That day in 2008 seemed to be the high mark of Brandon's career. There had never been another deal like it. In the years since then, profit margins had been leaner. There were, occasionally, quick deals or flips—like the one that I had witnessed—where he could make a tidy profit; but these, too, were becoming rarer. When I visited him, in early 2013, Brandon's situation seemed especially precarious. At the end of one workday, Brandon announced that the agency had earned just $900 and that he was going to the casino to replenish the company's coffers. Brandon also alluded to the fact that he owed money—not just to Aaron, but to some other business associate and the IRS as well. "Right now it just so happens that I'm in a bad spot," he told me. "But I made a lot of people a lot of money, in a lot of different ways. So I'm not as concerned about tomorrow, and I don't think [the people I owe] are, either. Obviously, they'd like to have it today. You know what I'm sayin'?"

Brandon did own a fair amount of property in Maine—including five houses and a farm—but he didn't own them outright. In fact, one afternoon when I was having lunch with him at a roadside stand, we met a middle-aged woman named Carol Harvey who was his real estate agent, mortgage broker, and banker all rolled into one. According to Brandon, his credit scores were so low that it would have been difficult for him to finance a traditional mortgage, so he went through Carol instead. She held the deed to the numerous properties that he owned, and he paid her each month instead of the bank. "We met him and fell in love with him—the good, bad, and the ugly," she told me.

"She has a little pet name for me," said Brandon. "It's Cocksucker."

"No, we don't say that," said Carol, laughing.

I was a little surprised that Carol and Brandon were on such good terms given what he had told me about his finances. Eventually, I asked Carol whether Brandon had missed any payments. Brandon did "get in trouble" occasionally, she said, and he had been late on some payments. "But he's honest with us. And then we say, 'Okay, let's work on this.'" While Carol spoke, it seemed as if she were echoing Aaron Siegel's very words, professing her faith in Brandon despite all of his missteps. She was also echoing Brandon's former boss, Jeff Schreiber, who hailed him as a bad boy turned good—a real-life Horatio Alger. Despite all the warning bells that he set off—or should have, rather—the way that he lived his life and spun his own tale made people want to believe in him.

The only person at Brandon's agency who seemed especially worried about finances was his bookkeeper. Her name was Shana Maloney, and she was also Brandon's stepdaughter. One afternoon, I wandered into an office tucked away in a corner of the agency and struck up a conversation with her. She was a pretty woman, in her mid-twenties, with shoulder-length blond hair. The walls of Shana's office were essentially barren except for a few letters tacked to the wall. They were utility bills for the office. I asked Shana what they were doing on the wall, and she said that they were unpaid because she didn't have the funds, and she was hoping that Brandon would notice them and appreciate the gravity of their situation. She tacked them to the wall on a whim, she explained. "I'm like, *I wonder if I just put these up and he sees them, will he feel the anxiety that I feel— and the stress?*"

Another problem, Shana explained, was that Brandon didn't collect a regular paycheck and sometimes simply used the debit card linked to the company's business account to cover his personal expenses. "He promised me the other day he's going to stop doing this," she told me. "He gave me the debit card, but he's done this before." Shana was used to Brandon's erratic behavior; after all, she had lived under the same roof as he had for years. "Once he gets an idea in his head, he just does it," she said. "He would get home at one a.m. and tell my mother, 'Wake up the kids. We're going camping.' And we would go." Shana stared up at the bills and shook her head. She seemed close to tears. "I'm the one seeing the bills that aren't being paid," she told me quietly. "It's like I almost have the fucking world on my shoulders and everybody else is oblivious."

Brandon may have exuded nonchalance, but he wasn't oblivious. Not at all. He understood, above all else, that he had to keep finding deals on paper. This was the key to turning a profit. He needed to do this as a debt broker; and he had to do this as the owner of a collection agency, because his collectors always needed new accounts to work. This need was complicated by the fact that there was simply less debt on the market. By early 2013, I got the sense that if he didn't acquire some paper soon—either to sell or to give to his own collectors—he might not be in business much longer. What he really needed to do was to find a great deal on a large quantity of debt. And quickly. The timing was crucial because tax refund season was rapidly approaching. This was the one time of year when even poor and working-class people had a little extra cash lying around. It was the equivalent of the holiday season for collectors when yearly net profits were either made or lost.

Fortunately, each and every February there was a place that Brandon visited to solve his problems—a happy hunting ground for paper—and that place was Las Vegas.

7

SCORING IN VEGAS

Once every February, more than a thousand debt buyers travel to Las Vegas to attend an annual conference sponsored by DBA International—which bills itself as a "nonprofit trade association" and "the voice of the debt buying industry." Aaron compared the scene with the bar in the movie *Star Wars*, where Luke Skywalker and Obi-Wan Kenobi met Han Solo. "You get all walks of life," he explained. For those serious about buying or selling paper, billions of dollars' worth at a time, for the lowest possible price—a nickel on the dollar, or a penny, or even one tenth of a penny—this is where you come. Much of the consumer debt that is bought and sold in the United States each year changes hands because of what happens here.

In 2013, the mood was subdued. Buyers from all over the country worried about a tightening market in which every opportunity had to be pursued. In particular, a great many were angling to purchase a large parcel of debt that everyone was calling the "Rincon paper." The FTC had recently shut down a large collection company known as Rincon Debt Management.

According to the FTC, Rincon employees had harassed debtors, threatened them with arrest, and sometimes even coerced them into paying debts that they didn't actually owe. The FTC had seized Rincon's paper and was preparing to auction it off through a court-appointed receiver. Brandon had heard rumors, however, that the Rincon paper was tainted. He wanted to learn more. And the key to doing this, it turns out, was to hang out in bars, casinos, and hotel lobbies.

The convention, which was held at the Aria Resort & Casino, had an official schedule, with lectures and workshops on new developments in the industry. But that's not really why Brandon came. Most debt buyers were in Las Vegas for the ten-minute meetings, which they attended in rapid succession. Theoretically, all of these interactions could have occurred over the phone, but in an industry with so little trust—where sellers worry about getting paid and buyers worry about what, exactly, they're buying—people still liked to meet in person.

On the first day of the convention, I arrived at the Aria to meet up with Brandon and accompany him to a number of meetings that he had scheduled. His first meeting was at 11:00 a.m., but as the time neared, Brandon was nowhere to be seen. In his stead was Jeremy Mountain, the young man who headed sales and compliance for the agency. On this particular morning, Jeremy and I waited patiently for Brandon to show up, until it became apparent that he wasn't coming.

"Where is he?" I asked finally.

Jeremy shrugged his shoulders and speculated: "Probably on a rampage yelling, 'Where is my weed?'" Jeremy went on to tell me that he typically did all the "bitch work" at conventions—waking up early, filling out the paperwork, and making sure that the company was properly accredited. He also often met prospective clients before Brandon did. "I'm like the professional façade of this corporation, and then I just pretty much loosen them up so they get a full grasp of what Brandon's going to be like," he told me.

"What do you tell them?"

"I say, 'Listen, he's a little bit unorthodox, but he's a good guy and you can go make money with him. You just got to get past the fact that he's probably highly intoxicated and swears like a sailor.'"

"Do you actually tell them this?"

"Yeah, kind of," he said with a laugh. Except he usually made his pep talk more professional, he added. Jeremy's goal, apparently, was simply to help Brandon consummate the deal. Aaron referred to Jeremy as "Brandon's fluffer"—a reference to the stagehand in pornographic movies who helps the male actor get aroused. Yet, in a way, Aaron often played a similar role, serving as an intermediary between Brandon and the sorts of people who might otherwise clutch their wallets tightly when passing Brandon in the hall.

Brandon never showed up for the 11:00 a.m. meeting, so Jeremy stood in for him and met with the debt buyers, two somber-faced men dressed in business attire, who seemed slightly irritated. "Where is Brandon?" one asked.

"He partied pretty hard last night," explained Jeremy apologetically.

"You're saying he hasn't emerged yet?" asked the buyer, glancing at his watch. "That's what you mean?"

"Yes."

"I see."

The meeting went on without Brandon.

Not long after this, I joined Jeremy for another meeting—this one with a short, soft-spoken man, who asked that I identify him by his nickname, "Elie." Elie was an Orthodox Jew who sported a thick beard, spectacles, and a yarmulke. Elie explained that he needed to hire an agency to help him work his paper, which was mainly payday loans. These loans are taken out by people in desperate need of cash and the interest rates are steep—annual rates typically are 391 percent. Payday loans are considered "scummy" paper, as one agency owner told me, because the balances are small and the debtors often don't pay or can't be found. Jeremy started giving his pitch, explaining what sort of man his boss was, when Brandon showed up.

Brandon was easy to spot from afar, since he was the only man in the lobby who didn't look like he had just stepped out of a glossy advertisement for Office Depot. He wore jeans, a checkered button-down shirt, and a black baseball cap emblazoned with a large white "B." He had heavy stubble on his chin, and he looked as if he hadn't slept much in the last few days. He introduced himself and took out a silver business-card case stenciled with his own initials, B.W., and the words PROBLEM SOLVER. He handed Elie a card. Jeremy quickly explained who Elie was and that he needed help collecting on some payday loans.

"I always look down on you payday-loan guys as scum, but now I'm begging for your crumbs because I have no paper," said Brandon.

Elie looked surprised, but not insulted.

"We are starving for inventory," Brandon continued. "Anything that you have on the back end, I'm interested in. We need inventory for collection and resale. Give us a test file. We'll collect and put it to sale at the same time."

"Where will you work it?" asked Elie.

"My agency."

Elie seemed hesitant. Not long ago, he said, he had been

cheated by an agency in Kentucky that never sent him the money that it owed him.

"How much do they owe you?" asked Brandon.

"A couple of thousand."

"Sometimes you have to take physical action," Jeremy said. Brandon nodded.

"They don't call me back and they won't pay me," said Elie.

"As long as they are not still collecting on that paper, you need to just write it off as a loss," Brandon said.

"What would you do?" asked Elie.

"Depends how mad I am," Brandon said, "and how much money it is." The bottom line, he explained, was that if he ever brokered a deal for Elie and one of the parties involved was a swindler, Brandon would personally give Elie the money that he was due. And then Brandon would handle the problem himself. This was, of course, the Brandon Wilson insurance program. Before rushing off to his next meeting, Elie promised to send Brandon a "test file." Brandon didn't look too thrilled, expressing doubts that Elie had enough paper to keep him busy; and, as it turns out, Elie never even sent over the test file.

Brandon still had the Rincon paper to look into, but in the meantime, he was on the hunt for other prospects. The market was tight, he said. The paper that was available was overpriced and was being snatched up by "the big guys"—five or six of the largest debt-buying companies. Everyone else was scrambling to make do. As Brandon continued chatting with various buyers and sellers, we bumped into Tom Borges. He was the broker whom I had visited in the summer of 2012 and who—upon discovering that some banks would limit the resale of credit-card debt—had pledged to "reinvent" himself.

Tom was a swaggering, immaculately groomed fifty-two-year-old man. His skin was deeply tanned and his hair gelled in slick spikes; a shiny silver hoop dangled from his left ear; and his clothing was so tight you'd expect the seams to burst if he flexed his bulging chest and torso muscles too vigorously. Tom is a legend in collections, an enduring figure who has been working as a collector, a debt buyer, or a broker for over three decades. In his early days, Tom ran a collection agency staffed largely by born-again Christians, whom he sometimes recruited at Bible study groups. Tom's collectors called debtors, listened to their woes, cried with them, prayed with them, and told them that they had to pay only 20 percent of the principal that they owed—moreover, 20 percent of what they paid would go to a Christian charity that helped feed the poor. In the test run for this program, Tom bought a portfolio of debt for $7,000 and collected $180,000 on it in roughly sixty days. In fact, according to Tom, this business model worked so well that he was soon approached by several leading evangelical figures who wanted to expand the size and the scope of the operation. In the end, Tom said that he became cynical about organized religion and decided to keep his business and his spirituality separate. Apparently, though, he still had a fondness for the religiously minded, because when it came to hiring his deputy, he recruited the principal of the Christian school that his children attended. Nowadays, Tom worked almost exclusively as a debt broker and had secured a reputation as a man supremely in the know about the ebb and flow of paper.

I knew Tom fairly well prior to seeing him in Las Vegas. I had spoken with him a number of times about the collections industry and, in the summer of 2012, had even spent several days hanging out with him at his Victorian mansion in Napa, California. During my visit, Tom had told me at length that the industry was changing and that his sources—insiders who worked closely with the banks—were all telling him that credit-card paper was becoming increasingly scarce. What's more, at least one bank—Chase—had suspended the sale of all credit-card debt. At the time, Tom was scrambling to acquire other types of paper, such as "cosmetic surgery debt." The sorts of debtors who got breast implants or face-lifts, he assured me, could ultimately pay 99 percent of the time. Tom was also acquiring pay-day loans. He explained that his clients could buy these loans, work them, and make a 30-percent return on their money in just sixty days. In any case, Tom had been hoarding as much paper as he could in anticipation of the imminent shortage.

Now, in Vegas, Tom seemed remarkably calm and composed as he greeted Brandon and lamented out loud that some banks were now stipulating that whoever bought their credit-card paper could *never* resell it.

"Really?" said Brandon, genuinely surprised.

"How do you like that shit?" asked Tom.

"Really?" Brandon repeated.

"Work it, but never [sell] 'til death do you part," Tom said, shaking his head. "So whatever's out there is what's left. That's why you're having a hard time finding anything."

"How we going to bust this open, Tom?"

"Well, we got a few buckets we can still pull out," Tom said reassuringly. There was still debt in his inventory, including $70 million worth of fresh paper from an agency that purchased directly from the banks. This particular portfolio of debt, apparently, had no restrictions about resale. "We're about ready to bring that to market," said Tom. "I'm sure you're going to be interested in that."

"Definitely," said Brandon.

"A lot of it's ninety-day-old paper," added Tom.

"I'm interested."

"I know you're interested," said Tom.

"I'm definitely interested."

"Yeah," said Tom, "I know."

There was, however, a catch to doing business with Tom. The catch was that Brandon, and all other would-be clients, had to sign a contract guaranteeing that after making an initial purchase from one of Tom's sellers, they would continue to use Tom as their broker for all subsequent deals with that seller. This was Tom's way of locking himself into an ongoing business relationship between a particular buyer and seller. "I call it handcuffing," Tom later told me, "because they are handcuffed to me for life." In truth, this wasn't all that different from the tactic that Brandon himself used when brokering for Aaron. Once he set up a deal, Brandon usually insisted on brokering all subsequent deals between the same two parties. In this scenario with Tom, Brandon would, in effect, be getting the Brandon treatment.

"That's how we make money, man," explained Tom.

"No doubt," said Brandon.

Brandon waved a friendly good-bye to Tom Borges and, moments later, told me that he would *not* be doing business with him. Not ever. "Borges wants to throw me off the scent," Brandon told me, almost in a growl. "Borges don't want me in there. He don't want me and my foot in the door because then I don't need Borges." The trick now, explained Brandon, was finding a "bucket" of older debt—the sort that had no preconditions from a bank.

I asked Brandon if the new preconditions, which he had just learned about, made him nervous.

"It doesn't make me nervous, cuz it doesn't change the status quo," replied Brandon, "and the status quo is there's no paper coming." At the end of the day, he added, it didn't really matter *why* there was a shortage. "It's like if [a guy] is dead and I say, 'Oh, he got hit by a car?' And then they're like, 'No, he got hit by a truck.' Well, what difference does it make, right? He's fucking dead and there's nothing we can do about it."

Eventually, Brandon and I met up with Aaron in the hotel's main lobby. Brandon pulled out his wallet, peeled off ten hundred-dollar bills from a thick wad of cash, and handed them to Aaron. Brandon was, apparently, slowly paying off what he owed. The transaction looked suspiciously like a drug deal, and several members of the Office Depot crowd exchanged befuddled glances and then resumed their conversations. Aaron and Brandon began discussing the Rincon paper and whether it was any good.

Brandon worried that the paper might be bad paper for a number of reasons. He suspected that after Rincon collapsed, a number of collection agencies hired by Rincon had continued to collect on the paper—illegally and very aggressively—and had pocketed whatever they made. Whoever bought that paper next, Brandon reasoned, could get hit with lawsuits from angry debtors as soon as they started trying to collect on it. Plus, the FTC would be keeping a close eye on what happened to the paper. And finally, there was the issue of the "chains of title" and whether or not there was hard-and-fast proof that Rincon had even owned this paper. Nonetheless, Brandon concluded, "Anything's good at the right price. There could be a profit, but I wouldn't pay more than two and a half bips." A bip, more formally called a basis point, is one hundredth of a penny. That means Brandon would offer no more than $102,500 for $410 million worth of debt that the FTC was selling. "That's like a low ball of a low ball [offer]," he said.

"That's what makes it so tempting for people that really don't know anything about business," said Aaron, shaking his head knowingly. "Like I can buy this for one tenth of a penny or less. How can I lose money?" Then he turned to me and added, "Guess what? *You can.*"

"Yeah, right, you can," said Brandon.

The Rincon paper was being auctioned off by a court-appointed receiver and with the aid of well-known debt broker named John Pratt, based in Ohio. According to his company, Portfolio Management Group, the FTC had examined the paper, sorted out the good from the bad, and was now selling some 248,000 accounts with a "face value" of $410 million. The paper was being sold on an "as is" basis. Pratt later told me that even he had not yet seen the actual chains of title for the Rincon paper because the FTC would release them only to the winner of the auction, after the sale. By industry standards, it was not that unusual to withhold the chains of title in this manner, said Pratt. He then added, "All the paperwork in this case was in storage somewhere."

"From the FTC's perspective," said Pratt, "they very rarely sell debt—they don't have the experience—so it wouldn't even be on their radar that there might be some bogus chains of title in the mix. But when I auction debt, I have to tell people this might be a possibility, in order to be transparent." In this case, Pratt's company was helping organize the auction and he himself was also bidding on the paper, which meant that he, too, was trying to determine how much it was worth. "This is the risk," said Pratt. "And this risk exists in all debt purchases."

Brandon's worst fears seemed to be confirmed the following day. In an open-air patio at the hotel, he and I bumped into a friend of his, a debt broker named Mattea Heldner. Mattea was in Las Vegas along with her son, a creditor's attorney named

Galen Hair who had, incidentally, gained quite a bit of attention at the convention for handing out condoms with his firm's internet address and two slogans: "Don't get screwed by consumer attorneys!" and "There's no need to pull out of the industry!"

Mattea told us that she had handled deals for Rincon in the past and she claimed to be intimately familiar with the paper that the FTC had seized.

"Did you bid on the Rincon stuff?" asked Mattea.

"I did not actually bid—but I was going to," replied Brandon.

"You should talk to me."

"I was only going to bid two and a half bips," said Brandon.

"Well, that's all I would have suggested," said Mattea, because it was "bad paper." Brandon nodded and confided what he'd heard about the paper, including the speculation that some of the files had been stolen.

"They were stolen after the offices had closed down," confirmed Mattea.

"Stolen—right. Exactly," said Brandon. This meant some of the paper was "tainted," Brandon said, and even though the auctioneers claimed to be selling only the nontainted paper, this was hardly reassuring.

Mattea agreed. She was skeptical that the FTC, or its court-appointed receiver, had been able to neatly separate the tainted paper from the untainted paper. There was simply too much paper and no easy way to sift through it carefully. As Mattea saw it, there were two potential problems affecting *all* the paper that Rincon owned. The first was that some of Rincon's paper had likely been stolen after the FTC shut down the company's operations. The second was that some of the "signed bills of sale"—proving Rincon's ownership—were missing because they had been "lost." Mattea was certain about this, she explained, because she had heard it directly from the owners of Rincon.

Later on, I tracked down John Pratt, who was helping organize the auction, and told him the gist of what Mattea had said. Pratt wasn't the least bit surprised, and told me that he knew Mattea well and that she was simply spreading malicious rumors in the hopes of sabotaging his auction. Pratt claimed that he and Mattea had been involved in a business dispute and now she was simply seeking to get back at him. "If you studied her for any length of time, you would see that she is a Wiccan witch and, in fact, she threatened to turn me into a frog once," he told me. "I forget if it was a frog or a toad." Mattea said that she had never done business with John and that this allegation was absurd. She acknowledged that she had been a Wiccan priestess since 1981, but explained, "I never threatened to turn anyone into a toad because that is just impossible. The tenet of my religion is not to hurt people. It is to celebrate nature and life."

I eventually went directly to the FTC and asked Chris Koegel, an assistant director in the Division of Financial Practices, about the integrity of the Rincon paper. He told me that he believed the paper was good, but then added, "Can I say with one-hundred-percent absolute certainty that somebody didn't steal some of the information and walk out the door with it, you know, independently? No, I can't. I have no idea what happened with every single employee that walked out that door." When it came to the quality and integrity of the paper that it was selling, neither the FTC nor the court-appointed receiver were willing to make any promises. In fact, the "purchase and sale agreement" stated explicitly that the "seller does not warrant in any manner whether all or any data, including but not limited to the balance, date of charge off, date of last payment and loan type, supplied to Purchaser is true and accurate."

At this point, I was rather dumbfounded. It seemed astounding to me that this was how the federal government was auctioning debt that it had seized. It was effectively admitting that the debt might have been stolen, prior to sale; what's more, it was refusing to make any guarantees about the debt itself. Equally astounding was that information about the worth of this paper was being determined by hearsay of theft, speculations about lost chains of title, and rumors of spells cast by witches.

"The whole thing just smells bad," Brandon concluded, in his conversation with Mattea.

"Right," she replied.

The chatter in the convention hall was squarely focused on the regulators. Everyone either seemed to be angling to buy the FTC's paper or speculating about whether the FTC—and its new companion, the Consumer Financial Protection Bureau—was going to shake up the industry. People spoke with dread of receiving a letter in the mail from the CFPB, announcing that an investigation or inquiry was under way. I heard one lawyer tell an audience of listeners that such a letter was a "nuclear bomb." "It will shut down everything," he said. "The first thing that will happen is you will get an absolute sense of panic." The fear that this might happen stemmed from the fact that—just one month earlier, in January 2013—the CFPB had officially begun to monitor the nation's largest debt-collection companies. This meant that a team of examiners from the CFPB could show up, any day, to scrutinize the business practices of one of these companies.

This was such a concern, apparently, that there was even an informational session for conventioneers: "Handling an FTC or CFPB Investigation." The panel's moderator was a well-respected former FTC lawyer—now in private practice—who quickly sought to reassure the audience: "Most of you, thankfully, will never go through an investigation." He went on to explain that the FTC conducted fewer than fifty investigations a year and that it pursued only the most egregious offenders. When it came to the CFPB, he assured the crowd that these new regulators were "just getting their toe in the water" and it would likely be some time before they would become "more of a threat." As of January 2013, the CFPB has the authority to supervise companies whose collection activities generate more than $10 million in annual receipts, which includes the nation's 175 largest players; and while the CFPB can also go after certain smaller companies, it says it will be focusing its attention almost exclusively on the big players. The problem is that there are 9,599 debt-collection businesses in the United States. In short, the CFPB's toe in the water remained at quite some distance from the industry's self-proclaimed bottom-feeders, like Brandon.

One afternoon, I went out for beers at the hotel bar with Aaron, Brandon, and one of Brandon's childhood friends from Boston, Ryan Vargus. Brandon still hadn't found any paper to buy, but he didn't seem overly concerned. I sat next to Ryan, a waifishly thin thirty-nine-year-old with a boyish face and a soft-spoken, easygoing manner. Ryan was quick to tell me that he had spent most of his adult life in prison. "I did fifteen years for weed," he said, with a casual shrug. He was charged with possession of 6,000 pounds. When he finally got out of jail, he decided to follow Brandon's lead and enter the collections industry, and Ryan and his wife now ran their own agency.

Ryan had come to Las Vegas in hopes of finding a new source for paper—namely, anyone other than Brandon. Brandon had been supplying Ryan with virtually all of his paper. Most of it was paper that Ryan purchased from Brandon, including portfolios that Aaron's fund had once owned. The rest of it was paper that Brandon either owned or controlled and that he allowed Ryan to collect on and earn a commission.

Autonomy is what Ryan wanted, and he hoped to secure it here in Las Vegas, by finding a new supplier. Oddly enough, Ryan claimed to have enjoyed a fair amount of independence during his time in prison. He told me that, while incarcerated, he ran an elaborate betting enterprise, where inmates could wager on professional sports teams. He employed ten different runners, from the prison's different blocks, who took the bets. On one occasion, Ryan recalled a gambler who tried to cheat him by placing a bet after a game had started. Ryan refused to honor his bet and eventually confronted him in the prison yard: "I stood my ground and went out there with a big old knife and said, 'I'm not paying it—that ain't how it works.'" According to Ryan, this kind of scenario was rare. Most of the time, inmates bet fairly and paid their debts. This was quite a contrast to the outside world, where collectors had to cajole debtors over the phone in the hopes that they *might* pay. All in all, prison provided Ryan with excellent training for running his own collections business: "You want to hit your goal, you want to cover your ass, and you don't want to collect less than what you're paying."

Aaron appeared enthralled by Ryan's tales from prison, and, at one point, he couldn't resist asking, "How long would I last in prison?"

Ryan eyed Aaron appraisingly for a moment, as if assessing his prison-worthiness. "You'd be fine," said Ryan finally. "The main thing is, you mind your business. You do your time. As long as you're not sucking a dick, doing drugs that you can't pay for, or gambling that you can't pay for, you're fine."

Ryan and Aaron both feared being too dependent on Brandon even as they worried about the risk of going elsewhere and buying bad paper from an unknown broker. The good side of dealing with Brandon, Ryan said, was that he never got "screwed." His other sources hadn't proved as reliable. He once purchased paper from another supplier and discovered that it was being worked, simultaneously, by seven other agencies. "What happened was, at some point down the line, the file had been outsourced to some scumbags," explained Ryan. "[Then they] sold it to a bunch of people, instead of returning the file to their clients like they were supposed to do." The takeaway from this story was clear: until he could find a more reliable supplier, Ryan was stuck with Brandon.

Later on, when I asked Brandon about Ryan's bid for independence, he replied, "I think once he gets around and checks prices, he'll come back, because people always think the grass is greener somewhere else." Ryan's real problem, Brandon insisted, was the quality of the collectors that he had in his office. "I'm giving this kid great deals," said Brandon. "He's getting it cheaper than all my regular customers because he's a friend of mine."

Aaron's and Ryan's relationships with Brandon were further complicated by their claims that Brandon owed them tens of thousands of dollars. To this end, Ryan said he was worried about Brandon's gambling. Ryan recounted how, one time, Brandon was driving down to see him with some money in hand, but en route he stopped at a casino and gambled it away. Brandon confirmed this. At one point, I listened as Aaron and Ryan discussed their prospects of getting repaid. Aaron speculated that Ryan was in the better position, and he went on to enumerate Ryan's advantages as a creditor, which included "geographic proximity," "longtime friendship," and the fact that "at the end of the day, when push comes to shove, [Ryan] is a little more intimidating."

"What's your recourse?" Aaron asked Ryan. "Where does the rubber meet the road?"

"I don't know," said Ryan, shaking his head. "I do not know."

The question of what Aaron, Brandon, and Ryan could—or couldn't—expect from one another because of friendship seemed to be an ongoing source of speculation. Business aside, Ryan and Brandon had remained deeply loyal to each other. During the time that Brandon was in prison, Ryan paid the mortgage on Brandon's mother's house so she could keep the home. Years later, when Ryan was nearing the end of his time in prison, Brandon sent him money each month so he could stay out of trouble and refrain from other, riskier means of making money.

One evening, I joined Aaron, Ryan, and Ryan's wife, Kaleigh, for dinner at the Palm. At the end of dinner, Ryan asked us politely, "Do you guys mind if we chew and screw? We got a show to catch." Aaron and I said that we didn't mind at all.

As he watched them leave, Aaron lamented that he didn't know more shady characters like Ryan, adding that it was important to "cultivate" such friendships. "Everyone knows accountants," he told me.

Aaron went on to say that, no matter what crimes Ryan or Brandon had committed, they seemed to have a bond that endured in the way that many of his own friendships and business relationships never would. He recalled his sense of misery and isolation when he was going through the painful divorce from his first wife. "Brandon would call me up and ask me, 'Aaron, how are you doing?' He was really concerned. Some of my friends from Buffalo, they really weren't there for me." For a moment, Aaron's eyes glazed over with tears. "Don't get me wrong," he said. "It's not that Brandon wouldn't mark up the price on a file—but that's all fair game."

At times, it was clear that Aaron romanticized Brandon's code of honor. Sensing that, Brandon seemed to ham it up, playing the role of the noble outlaw to his own advantage. But the romanticizing cut both ways. It often appeared that Brandon took pride in the idea that someone like Aaron, with such an aura of wealth and respectability, considered him such a close friend. Brandon was touched when Aaron once invited him to attend a political fund-raiser at Herb Siegel's house. It was a big event and Bill Clinton was scheduled to attend. "I was very happy that I was even in a position to be invited to something like that, because, you know, coming from where I come from, that doesn't happen much," said Brandon. In the end, Brandon worried that his criminal past might somehow embarrass Aaron and Herb, so he opted not to go. Afterward, when Brandon explained why he hadn't shown up, Aaron said that no one would have cared about Brandon's past: they would have accepted checks from *anybody*.

Brandon finally found his paper—or a good lead on it, anyhow—the following morning in the hotel casino. We were headed toward a bank of slot machines when a heavyset, ruddy-faced man in a golf shirt approached us. The man, who was Brandon's old acquaintance, pulled him aside and told him about a $600 million portfolio of credit-card paper that one of the big debt-buying companies was looking to unload. The debt was on the older side—it was unclear, at this point, just how old—but the acquaintance knew that Brandon liked to work older, beaten-up paper that no one else typically wanted. The banks had charged off and sold this paper before imposing any of the new preconditions, which meant it could be sold and resold indefinitely.

Brandon's immediate challenge was paying for this particular portfolio of debt. Brandon speculated that it could cost him as much as twenty basis points—or one fifth of a penny on the dollar—and this meant that Brandon needed to line up as much as $1.2 million in capital right away. Normally, he would turn to Aaron in this situation; but at this point, Aaron didn't have the cash on hand or the inclination to make such a big investment. Instead, Brandon he would ask an old friend and business associate, who asked to be identified by his middle name, George.

George was a former collector, who had opened his own agency and done very well for himself. The secret to George's success, Brandon explained, was that he always held on to his "postdates"—these were accounts connected to debtors who had agreed to set up extended payment plans, in which they paid $25 or $50 a month for several years. Brandon, by contrast, often sold his postdates at a discount to get a lump sum of cash as quickly as possible. He had done this, just several months earlier, in order to pay off the bulk of a debt that he owed to Aaron. The strategy, Brandon admitted, was effective but short-sighted: "I was always like, nah, I ain't going to be here for those postdates—just give me the fifty [thousand] right now."

"I run out of cash once a month," Brandon told me. "I run out of cash and I turn to him." Brandon seemed certain that George would come through. "When my chips are down and I got no one to turn to, and I can't go make fifty grand tomorrow to pay, I turn to him."

George's hotel room was a sprawling, multiroom penthouse with breathtaking views of the Las Vegas skyline and the desert landscape beyond. By the time I arrived, a party was well under way. The minifridge appeared to be plundered—small bottles of liquor were scattered everywhere—and a thick cloud of cigarette and marijuana smoke lingered in the air. A dozen or so people were there, including Brandon, Aaron, Ryan, and his wife.

A friendly, heavyset fellow in shorts and a T-shirt—who turned out to be George—introduced himself and told me that he had come to Las Vegas to do a little business, gamble, and attend his best friend's wedding. George helped foot the bill for his friend and his friend's fiancée to make the trip. The friend appeared quite appreciative and referred to George as "the King." Now the King was making plans to attend a concert while simultaneously listening to Brandon brief him on the deal that he had lined up. The paper was eight to fifteen years old, Brandon explained, with charge-off dates ranging from 1997 to 2005. "George, they got a massive inventory," said Brandon. "It's a publicly traded company, George. They only want to deal with me."

I asked George if he had any concerns about the deal. George told me that as long as the paper wasn't "bogus"—meaning it hadn't been double-sold and the chain of title was legitimate—he felt confident he would make money. Plus, George added, Brandon always took care of any problems that arose. The previous fall, for example, Brandon helped broker a deal for George involving a portfolio of payday loans. George quickly discovered that the accounts he had purchased were not legitimate, but merely the names and social security numbers of people who had applied for payday loans in the past. Brandon reimbursed George and then set out to solve the problem. He didn't bother contacting the FTC, which would likely have done little good. Ultimately, he flew down to Miami in search of "the kid" who had sold him these files, but couldn't find him. "The kid is in the wind," Brandon told me. "I wish I knew where he was right now. I would take a taxicab over there and smash his face in so he can't talk shit for six to eight weeks." The bottom line for George, however, was that Brandon had protected his investment.

"Here's the deal," Brandon said to George. "They only want to give it to one person—and they already chose me."

"Then just tell [him] I got all the money," George said. "He don't have to go anywhere else."

As the party continued in George's penthouse, Brandon began trying to convince Aaron to invest with him. Ryan, who was sitting across the table from the two of them, listened but said nothing.

"Aaron, all I need is one million dollars," said Brandon, in his excited voice—a full-throated yell. "In six months I can get you a fifty-thousand-dollar remit for the rest of your life."

"It's tough to get investors to put money in these days," Aaron said.

"Fuck the investors," Brandon shouted. "What about you?"

"I don't have a million dollars."

Brandon shot him a dubious look.

Someone across the room asked Brandon to talk more softly.

"I'm rude, crude, and socially unattractive," Brandon replied. "My balls dropped when I was eight."

Moments later, his cell phone rang.

"Here we go," he shouted. "Hotline—B.W. problem solver." Brandon paused to listen, then asked out loud what the room number for the penthouse was.

"Thirty-one thirty," someone shouted.

Brandon put the phone down and explained that another

potential deal was materializing. The owner of a large collection agency would soon be paying them a visit. The owner, Steve, apparently had the ability to put Brandon in touch with some of his clients who had large volumes of paper to sell. Business appeared to be rolling. As soon as Steve arrived, Brandon rose to his feet and barked, "I want to talk to some of your clients!"

"If you won't yell at them, I'll let you talk to them," said Steve. Brandon appeared satisfied.

Not long after this, a security guard arrived, explaining that someone had complained about the noise coming from this particular penthouse.

"Want me to deal with this?" shouted Brandon. "I'm a problem solver!"

Several people quickly intervened, assuring Brandon that this wasn't necessary.

As all of this transpired, I saw Ryan silently nodding his head. He had been sitting there so quietly that I had barely noticed him. He still hadn't found a new source of paper. His expression was blank, and I couldn't tell whether he was annoyed, amused, or ambivalent that Brandon had seemingly found good paper and was now bragging about it.

Brandon looked at his old friend and smiled warmly. "I got an eleven-to-fourteen-year sentence when I was a young kid, right?" said Brandon thoughtfully. Brandon had a startling ability to downshift his energy levels rapidly, so that he could go from Viking-battle-cry mode to introspective-philosopher mode and then back in a matter of seconds. "My father died in 1994, and my mother had a small nervous breakdown when my father died. *This kid*, right here, paid my mother's mortgage for like two years—even after he went to prison."

"I was in jail paying for it," Ryan confirmed, his face still blank.

"He was in jail sending my mother and my girl . . ." Brandon paused for a moment. Not everyone in the room was listening, and this seemed to irk him. "Hey!" shouted Brandon. Conversation dropped to a murmur. Then he resumed. "Sending my mother and girl fucking twelve hundred dollars a month. After he was already in prison. How many guys are going to do that?"

Brandon pointed to George and said, "I had a couple problems, and George stepped up and said, 'Brandon, if something happens to you, don't worry, I'll take care of your wife and kids.'"

George nodded appreciatively.

The room was fairly quiet now. Brandon was on a roll and no one was going to compete with him. It wasn't that everyone deferred to him obsequiously, as if he were a rock star entitled to their respect and love solely by his sheer charisma. Rather, Brandon created the impression that he was a charging bull, a creature whose sheer force was so brutal and overpowering that you had to move the hell out of the way once he got going. Sure, he was hamming it up, inflating himself into the caricature of the brash armed robber who had done "ten years in the can," but even this performance was part of the deal. This was his shtick, his talk-off, his chest-thumping war dance. And as loud, lewd, and unbearable as he could be, everyone seemed to believe that you needed a Brandon Wilson to scare off all the con men, hucksters, and charlatans in this industry. You needed a guy who had survived in the prison yard in order to help you succeed in a rude business. And if he was a little out of control, a little erratic, a little dangerous, then all the better. Because he was the great Boston alpha male, here to make a buck and keep the wolves at bay. Brandon was no fool—quite the opposite. He was a quick study. On some level, he understood the role that was expected of him, and he played it to the hilt.

"This is my guy, that's my guy, this is my guy, that's my guy over there," Brandon said, as he looked around the room and pointed at people. "Right? You know what I'm saying? And I'm going to tell you right now, if any one of these guys called me and said, 'I'm in trouble and I need you right now,' I would fucking come—money or no money."

"Would you come with a shovel?" someone yelled out, goading him on.

"You already know I'd come with a fucking shovel if that's what we needed," replied Brandon. "But I would be there. And you know what? I'm a man of my word, so that's what it's about. That's what it's about."

PART THREE

THE LAST COLLECTORS

8

TAKING CONTROL OF ASSETS

For all its roguish color, Las Vegas is the legitimate face of the debt-buying industry. It is the place where everyone—from the small operators to the big publicly traded debt buyers—comes to do business. Back on the streets of Buffalo, the rules are looser and the game is tougher. This is the *other* marketplace for consumer debt in America. It was here that the Package was stolen and here that paper of dubious origin is routinely bought and sold, no questions asked. For these reasons, it made sense to spend some more time in Buffalo. I still had a number of questions about the fate of the Package, and if I could answer them, I could understand what happened to debts—like Joanna's and Theresa's—when they dropped off the edge of the aboveground economy. I wanted to know just how far collectors would go to collect on the most "beaten-up" paper. In short, I wanted to know the inner workings of the financial underworld.

My usher into this realm was a Buffalo-based debt broker named Larry. I met Larry for the first time in the summer of

2012, at a bar on Chippewa Street, which was once the epicenter of Buffalo's theater district. Nowadays, Chippewa is where twenty-somethings, often from the suburbs, come to get drunk and gyrate to the pulse of the city's nightclubs—places with names like Bottoms Up, Bada Bing Bar & Grill, and Pure Night Club. Larry emerged from the crowd of revelers—a man dressed entirely in black. He wore dark sunglasses, black pants, a matching shirt, and a black Yankees cap, which gave him the air of a chic grim reaper. Larry was a youthful-looking African-American man in his mid-forties. He sported a diamond earring and a beard trimmed so finely that, if you saw his picture, you'd swear it was airbrushed.

Larry was, at heart, an artist. On and off, throughout his working life, he had survived on his art—making greeting cards, T-shirts, sculptures, and paintings. This was what he loved to do, but it never paid especially well; and so, when it came to making money, Larry had relied on buying and selling debt. He did this from wherever he was—in his house, in his car, or from a restaurant.

"You don't have to have an office to buy and sell," he told me, as we sat down at a bar with a sidewalk patio. "You just got to have a means to view the file. If you have a means to view it and pass it on, that's all you need. I keep all my paperwork on an SD [secure digital] card and just slip it right into my phone." He ran his fingers across his cell phone. "I got a virtual office in my hand."

One of the many reasons that I was curious to talk with Larry is that he claimed to be a former partner of the notorious debt broker named Kenny. When Brandon confronted Bill at the corner store, it was Kenny whom Bill fingered as the source of the stolen Package, though he'd later retract the claim. This explanation didn't surprise Brandon in the least. As Brandon put it, "Saying that Kenny sold you some bad paper and ripped you off is like saying, 'Guess who robbed me in the forest? Robin Hood!' Of course he did." Kenny did not return my calls but Larry proved to be eager to speak. He insisted that he himself hadn't handled the Package, but said it was entirely possible that Kenny had, because this was how business worked in their niche of the industry. Then he suggested that we meet in person, which is how we ended up on Chippewa Street.

As we sipped our drinks, and SUVs packed with partiers began to arrive, Larry told me that he was semiretired and now lived a quiet, middle-class life in the suburbs, where he spent his days painting. This was a return to the kind of stable, secure life that he had known as a young child. Larry was born into a decidedly middle-class family; throughout the 1960s, and much of the 1970s, his father had a good job at Bethlehem Steel. Then the steel mill shut down and everything fell apart for Larry.

Even now, more than thirty years later, Larry remembered with startling clarity the day from his childhood when his dad got laid off. "Dad came home, and he told my mom, 'Well, the plant decided to close.' [They] didn't give him notice. Actually, he was given notice, but maybe it kind of slipped his mind somehow. My dad's straight from the South, man, the Deep South—didn't have a whole lot of schooling. When he came home, he told us, 'You know what, we may have to sign up for social services.' At that time it wasn't called 'social service,' he just straight up said, 'We may have to go on welfare for a while.' I was like, 'No way,' because we teased the kids in school that were on welfare. And it was crushing. And I was like, 'Man, I don't wanna go to school, I don't wanna go outside, I don't wanna do anything.'"

After this, as Larry recalls it, he and his three siblings were always taking odd jobs and fending for themselves. "We bought our own school clothes, we bought our own school supplies, paid for our own haircuts—only thing we needed our parents for was to keep the roof over our head." Looking back, Larry says there were moments when it looked like he might beat the odds and succeed—like the time in high school when he won an essay-writing contest and, as a result, briefly landed a job at a local bank. But it didn't work out in the end. "I had friends that were into the streets, and they were making good money, and I had gotten to a point where I lost my job and I wasn't doing so well. So the next thing, I was selling drugs." Larry spent six of the next fifteen years in prison on a number of charges, including attempted robbery, attempted arson, and possession of a controlled substance.

"I've lived a very crazy life," said Larry. "It's been positive and negative, but I like where I'm at now. Very quiet, peaceful. I'm in total, one-hundred-percent control of my emotions. That's what the problem was. I had to learn that."

After getting out of prison, Larry met up with Kenny—who was an old friend of his from childhood—and Kenny helped him get a job at a large collection agency where he was working. They spent several years there, until they decided to venture out on their own and open a small firm that bought and sold debt. Larry actually said he made less money as a broker than a collector, but like Aaron, he found buying and selling debt far less stressful than having to collect on it. It also gave him freedom to travel and make his art. But dealing debt also soon proved to be a source of stress because, as Larry put it, many of his deals were "not legitimate."

By legitimate deals, Larry meant those in which the debt had a proper chain of title—much like a chain of title on a used car or a house—which indicated who the seller was and who the buyer was. Such a document served as legal proof that the owner was, in fact, the owner. When buying or selling legitimate debt, one wanted as much documentation as possible. "As a businessman, for your own personal protection, you want a money trail," Larry explained. Typically, one created such a trail by using attorneys, or a written contract, or by wiring money from bank to bank. These, in fact, were the sorts of deals that Brandon made. Brandon may have played the part of the freewheeling, street-hustling vigilante, but he only bought and sold debt with legitimate chains of title. This was a point of pride for him. As far as Brandon was concerned, the other sorts of deals—where there was no bona fide chain of title—were the work of the "sharks" whom he despised. In these "illegitimate" transactions, the broker might be double-selling a file, or selling a stolen file, or perhaps he was simply offering a file whose origin he didn't know and didn't *want* to know. Either way, it was necessary when making these deals to be more clandestine and not leave a paper trail.

"I've done deals where I met guys down here," said Larry, pausing to gesture down the street, "right down at the steakhouse down there—done a deal right in the car." In such cases, the buyer gave Larry cash, and he handed the buyer a thumb drive with a spreadsheet containing the names, addresses, social security numbers, credit-card balances, or loan amounts of several thousand debtors. Sometimes there was an informal one-page contract, but not always.

Where exactly, I inquired, were these files coming from? "I'm not asking where the files are coming from," he told me. "I'm just dealing." For Larry, this was simply commerce. He bought and sold thumb drives with data. For a moment, it all sounded so normal; and then, in the next instant, I remembered that this data belonged to people like Joanna and Theresa. What would they say if they knew that their personal information, including their debts, was being bought and sold on street corners like illegal drugs?

As it turns out, one of Larry's most loyal customers was a former cocaine dealer named Jimmy. Larry told me that when he met Jimmy, they connected immediately because they had similar backgrounds. Jimmy understood the implicit rules of making illegitimate deals. "That's another thing I respect about Jimmy," explained Larry. "Certain things you don't want to know, because once you know something, then you become an accessory to it or responsible—so it's just better not to know, because most of the dealings on the level that we're on, they're not legitimate."

The problem with all of this, said Larry, was that this mode of operating had become a lawless free-for-all. "Just over the last eight years there's been an explosion of street people coming into collections," he said. "You got guys literally coming out of prison today and next week they got a collection agency." According to Larry, there were hundreds of agencies being started by such "street people," and they were "doing deals in all kinds of funky ways," including buying debt that was double-sold and triple-sold.

"There's three agencies up here run by three guys that got out of prison—*right up here*," he said gesturing to a nearby building. "And they're surviving, man, so there's no one centralized local source—legitimate source—where they can come to and purchase their portfolios."

"Why not?"

"Nobody's big enough, man. Nobody's big enough." What

the city needed, said Larry, was one centralized outlet where collectors could buy legitimate debt. "That's why if I had a huge amount of paper, a big abundance of paper, we'd sell this city up. We'd own this city, man."

"To be honest with you, I haven't really been doing a lot of buying and selling debt because there's no more good debt around to sell that I was able to get my hands on," he told me. "I like legitimate deals." I asked him if he would like to work for a broker or agency that dealt exclusively in legitimate debt. "Yes!" he said. "Man, come with it. Come with some actual, factual paperwork! I want a real nondisclosure agreement that you're gonna honor. I'm gonna enforce it! I'm gonna make you honor it, and the deal is gonna go accordingly like it should. You'll look at a masked [encrypted] file, you'll want it or you don't want it, and then you'll forward over the money and you'll get your file. Just that simple. It'll be a legitimate file with a chain of title, showing you where it originated from. Yes, that's the thing!"

The problem, he added, was that there were always the people who wanted "to buy the files for super cheap" on the street. "That's really it," he concluded. "You get what you pay for. If you don't want to pay the thirty or forty grand that it costs for a great, legitimate file, then go ahead and pay three or five grand for a file without chain of title that's been triple-sold or ten times sold. Go ahead and take that chance. And that's what they're all doing. They're saying, 'We'll take the chance.'"

Larry sighed heavily. He looked tired and slightly disgusted. "I'm just distancing myself from the big money now, and I don't care. If I have to stay living a humble life and sell my little paintings, I'm fine. I'm not starving—there's food in my refrigerator."

Larry said he held on to the hope that, someday, he might work for or even own an agency that did things by the books—as they should be done. But he wasn't optimistic that this would happen. In his view, the "street people" flooding the industry had ruined things and given the entire city a bad name: "People look at Buffalo like a germ." And it wasn't just the city that bore this stigma. "Now it's hard to get a relationship with anybody, and to keep it all real, especially being black, nobody's gonna want to deal with you," he told me as he finished off his beer. "And I don't blame them—like this one time, I can't blame them, man."

Not long after I met Larry for drinks, I heard about a barber on the East Side of Buffalo who allegedly had been selling bad paper, inspiring two disgruntled customers to come back with guns and shoot up his barbershop. The East Side is filled with tiny shops that collect on debt. It doesn't take much to launch such a business: real estate is cheap, paper is readily available if you don't care about its pedigree, and the city has a huge labor pool of experienced collectors—many of whom are hungry for work. This particular barbershop was located in a rough area. In fact, during my relatively brief visit, the police descended on the block and arrested two women after one sliced the other with a broken-off bottle.

There was a security camera hanging over the front door of the barbershop, and I had to be buzzed in before I could enter. The barber denied that anyone had ever attacked his store, saying only that he had been robbed repeatedly. He also denied ever buying or selling debt, though he did say, rather cryptically, "I know some companies that help clean up people's credit." If I really wanted to know more about the debt business, he told me, I should walk down the block and visit another barber, named Sean.

Sean's barbershop was a cavernous mirrored hall, adorned with bright lights and ceiling fans and packed with young men waiting to get their hair cut. Sean wore shiny silver glasses, a thick chain around his neck, and a black barber's shirt with his shop's logo. He was a slightly built man, both friendly and garrulous. When I mentioned that I had been interviewing the barber down the street, Sean replied, "He does illegal things with people's credit—he does . . ." Then he stopped himself, as if suddenly remembering that he didn't actually know me, and finished, "I don't know what he's doing."

Sean went on to explain that, up until recently, he had been dabbling in the financial world. "Technically I would be called a 'position swing equities trader,'" he told me. This meant, it turned out, that he bought, sold, and collected debt—mainly payday loans. This industry was both profitable and shady, said Sean. He then recounted a story about a woman from Virginia who sold him a portfolio and threw in an additional file as a freebie. The woman didn't actually own the freebie, Sean said, but she had access to the file.

According to Sean, the freebie file was tainted—and thus a little harder to collect on—because the debtors had either already paid their debts or were currently being hounded by another agency that was working the same paper. "I knew it was tainted," he told me. "So I told all my collectors, 'Just run it.'" It was difficult to get debtors to pay a debt a second time, Sean said, but if a given debtor didn't have the paperwork to prove that they had already paid off the debt, then they still owed it. On this particular file, he needed to create a better incentive for his employees, so he increased the collectors' bonuses by 5 percent and the managers' by 10 percent. That's how you work a tainted file, he told me. But Sean was quick to say that he had generally avoided buying or working tainted paper and had done so on only two occasions.

I interviewed other collectors in Buffalo who also described the practice of buying, selling, and collecting on the accounts of debtors who had already paid their loans—mainly payday loans again. This was all apparently part of the trade of bad paper. One veteran collector, who had spent eight years working at a number of agencies in the Buffalo area, told me she once started working a new portfolio and realized that 95 percent of the accounts had already been paid. This is how she handled the situation: "You call them and you say, 'We're calling you about a payday loan you had back in 2006 for fifteen hundred dollars.' Then the person would say, 'Oh, I paid that payday loan off. I made a settlement of eight hundred with the company.'" At this point, the collector would say that this amount did not include interest and service fees—a boldfaced lie. But it worked. "So those people think, *Oh. I didn't pay that. I just paid the general principal* . . . So they'll pay it again." This same collector also told me that many of the collection agencies that bought, sold, and worked bad paper were funded, at least initially, with the proceeds from the sale of illegal drugs, mainly crack. She claimed to personally know six collection agency owners who got into the business that way. That wasn't the only interaction between drug dealers and the business. As she recalled, "I've seen other big-time drug dealers come to collection agencies and extort them, saying, 'Hey, I heard this shop is runnin' well. Everybody's drivin' brand-new Escalades and Jaguars. You got money. I need ten percent.'" All of this seemed to corroborate the rather dark, chaotic, and lawless assessment of the city's rogue agencies that Larry had given me.

Back at Sean's barbershop, I asked him why he had recently decided to retire from the business. He said the industry was simply too stressful and suspect. The collectors who made him money were typically the ones who were willing to intimidate debtors and break the law. And, of course, there were the tainted files. "Being a young man, who is a believer, I didn't like making my money that way."

I wanted to see Larry's artwork—I genuinely did—and I also wanted to question him more closely about the fate of the Package, so I decided to visit him at his house in an overwhelmingly white, working-class community outside of Buffalo. When I showed up at his home, a modest ranch house on a quiet side street, Larry greeted me excitedly and escorted me into his one-car garage, which he uses as his studio. It was a cramped, dark space cluttered with an old treadmill, a bench press, a television set, and other items that looked as if they were waiting to be sold at a yard sale. And there were art supplies, lots of them, including canvases, oil paints, brushes, jars of pumice, vials of crackle powder, and tubs of plaster of Paris.

Larry told me that he had chosen to live here, in the suburbs, to escape his past: "I actually wanted to go somewhere where there weren't a lot of black people. When you embrace change, you change everything. People, places, and things." But there were some drawbacks. "Like, if I say hello to someone, I'll just get no reply or just a crazy look and they'll keep walking—like, 'Don't speak to me, nigger, keep it going, you shouldn't even be around here.' That's the feeling I get."

This wasn't a big problem, Larry said, because most of the time he simply stayed inside, working on his art. He showed me one of his works in progress, which was an image of a human head, with images of a car, a stack of money, and a diamond placed above it. "The name of this painting is *Taking Control of Assets*, and what it's basically showing is a responsible guy who's thinking about what to do with his money," Larry said. "He's putting the money into assets that he can get his return back on later if he needs it." I asked what inspired the painting. "All of my paintings are extensions of my fears," he replied. "And what inspired me to do this is that I don't want to waste money. I don't want to squander it." Larry looked around his cramped studio, smiled, and then exhaled heavily. "I fear making bad decisions," he said quietly. "Like every day I'm working on me. How can I get better? How can I do this better? How can I do the right thing? Okay, if I get an impulse thought, don't react on it. Sit down. Think it over first. See if it's the best decision. I just fear making bad decisions."

Eventually, we got to talking about the Package and how it might have gotten into Bill's hands. Bill and Kenny had an ongoing relationship, said Larry, and it was entirely plausible that Kenny had sold him these accounts. But how, I pressed, would Kenny have obtained the accounts in the first place? Larry seemed amused by this question. He insisted there were countless ways and outlined several possibilities. One scenario was that Kenny simply bought the file from someone else not knowing—or wanting to know—where it came from. In another scenario, Aaron might have sent a portfolio to an agency that couldn't handle the volume. "A lot of agencies lie about the number of collectors they have," said Larry. Agencies do this because they are hungry for paper, and if they end up getting too much of it, they can then farm it out to another agency. In this scenario, an overwhelmed agency may have asked Kenny to help with their excess paper; and maybe Kenny did help, but on the side, he slipped a few accounts to Bill surreptitiously. A third scenario was that someone at one of Aaron's agencies stole the file and gave it to Kenny, at which point Kenny gave it to Bill, who tried to collect on it as quickly and as aggressively as possible, until someone noticed.

Larry didn't seem to know—or want to know—which of these scenarios, if any, was true. And I understood why. In this world, it was the knowing that implicated you. Speaking directly with Bill didn't clear anything up either. When I interviewed him, in 2013, he claimed not to recall implicating Kenny, but said that if he did so, it was only to throw Brandon off the trail. Bill claimed that he bought the accounts from someone at Franklin Asset, who he increasingly suspected was "doing some funny shit" with the accounts "behind Aaron's back." In the end, the many possibilities were both endless and dizzying in their complex permutations.

Yet even if it was impossible to know exactly *how* the paper had gotten into Bill's hands, I still wanted to learn more about the manner in which his shop, and others like it, operated. As it turned out, one of Larry's favorite clients, Jimmy (the former cocaine dealer), had worked as the office manager at Bill's shop and had then gone on to open his own collection agency, which was—in many ways—a replica of Bill's. I knew Jimmy because we had briefly gone to school together as kids, and I had already interviewed him about the collections industry. So I called him to arrange a meeting. Jimmy was eager to talk and suggested that we take a drive over to the old factory complex where Bill's shop had been located, just before it shut down.

9

THE WHITE MAN'S DOPE

Jimmy is an imposing figure. He dresses in low-slung pants, wears earrings in both ears, and has DADDY tattooed across his right arm. When he walks, he does so in a deliberate, powerful, plodding way, almost like a bear. But he isn't slow: one of Jimmy's proudest moments was captured by a video camera at a local corner store. The video shows him hustling out of the store, chasing down a criminal trying to steal his car, and then whipping open the driver's door and throwing the thief from the car. The incident was later immortalized on YouTube when someone posted the video under the heading "Want to steal a car but can't drive it." Jimmy exudes toughness. One of his former high school English teachers told me that even though Jimmy is "very, very bright" and has a broad, inviting smile, many teachers were "scared to death of him."

When I met up with Jimmy, we soon got to talking about Bill. Jimmy had worked with Bill for roughly a year, back in 2008, and he offered to give me a tour of their old office complex and tell me about all the details of the business. Only we didn't go there—not right away, anyhow. Instead, we took a meandering drive through the Bailey-Delavan neighborhood where he grew up. Jimmy likes any excuse to take a drive. He spends much of his waking hours in his car, driving around the city, because it invigorates him. He likes to be "just a stone's throw away from what's on the other side of the glass," because seeing the streets reminds him that "this is exactly where I'll be if I don't collect."

Bailey-Delavan is one of the poorest neighborhoods in Buffalo. Weeds grow knee-high in abandoned lots, trash cans are chained to walls, and many storefronts are shuttered. Two signs hang boldly in the local real estate office window, one advertising foreclosed homes and the other warning that the premises are shotgun protected. The neighborhood's architectural treasure, a Renaissance-style basilica called St. Gerard's, was closed several years ago; a group from Georgia plans to disassemble it, brick by brick, and ship its parts to a suburb of Atlanta, where it will be rebuilt. Over the past few decades, as more steel mills, grain elevators, and railroad yards became dormant, roughly half the city's population fled, and now even its buildings are headed south.

On almost every block, street signs were adorned with wilting flowers, deflated balloons, and weathered teddy bears. Also attached to these signs were plaques hand-painted with the names of someone who had died. "This is a killer block," Jimmy told me as we drove down a street with an especially large number of markers. "This is where you get buried and done off." Jimmy honked the horn and waved out the window at a guy standing on the corner. "What up, baby?" he yelled. I asked Jimmy who the guy was. "That nigger is a fucking murderer . . . All these little motherfucking niggers around here is—it's treacherous, dog."

Jimmy grew up in Bailey-Delavan and was raised almost entirely by his mother, Patricia—a devout Christian who made her living as a courtroom stenographer. Jimmy's father was a lifelong heroin addict. As a kid, Jimmy remembered running into the kitchen and glancing down the stairs into the basement, where his father was shooting up. Jimmy stood there, transfixed, watching him nod off. "He was like an extra kid that my mom took care of," Jimmy said. His mother would bring home what she earned, and, late at night, Jimmy would watch his father rifle through her purse and steal whatever he could. Sometimes there would be no money to light or heat the house. The family just barely survived, said Jimmy, mainly thanks to food stamps.

One of the few truly happy and lighthearted memories that he had from childhood was going to visit his grandmother, who worked as a maid at a large mansion on Middlesex Avenue—not too far from where Aaron Siegel had grown up. On these visits, no one ever told him that his grandmother worked there as a maid. Jimmy thought it was *her* house. After all, she had a room upstairs, where she sometimes stayed. And the white children, who lived at the house, even called her "Grandmomma," just as Jimmy did.

By the time Jimmy had turned nineteen, he was dealing large quantities of cocaine. He was adamant, however, that none of his siblings follow in his footsteps. His unsaid motto was *Do as I say, not as I do*. He insisted that his siblings study hard, stay off the streets, and go to college. And the plan ultimately worked. One of his siblings became a social worker and another is the deputy superintendent of a school system in a midsize American city. Jimmy used some of the money that he made on the streets to support his mother and his siblings, so his work served a practical purpose. But he also loved the work itself.

"Passion is when you love something so much you blinded by it," he told me. "I loved these streets so much and was so good at it." Or, as he told me on another occasion, he knew the East Side of Buffalo so well that someone could "fart over there and I'm going to tell you who did it." He began making so much money, he says, that he had to bury it in stashes around the city. He also spent it extravagantly. The first football game he ever went to was the Super Bowl—and he went, he recalled, in a hired limousine that drove him all the way from Buffalo to Atlanta.

Though he loathed his father for becoming a drug addict, Jimmy had become a dealer, a person who enabled addictions. And the irony wasn't lost on him either. One day he went to see his father, who was ill after shooting up "bad dope," as Jimmy put it. His father had become so sick that he had fallen out of bed and couldn't climb back in. "He was sitting there in his underwear, and he had peed on himself," recalled Jimmy. "So I'm looking at him like, 'Dad, man, you all right?' And he kind of gave me a grunt and a moan like 'Uhhhh.' I don't know what he was saying, but my phone kept going off." As the call from a client continued to ring, Jimmy knelt down to pick up his father, and his hefty gold necklace swung down, dangling in his father's face, obscuring their ability to see each other. And this is the last enduring memory Jimmy has of his father because he died later that very day.

Eventually, Jimmy was arrested on a felony gun charge. He says he was lucky that this was the only charge against him. Jimmy served six months at the Erie County Correctional Facility, in Alden, New York. Upon his release, he took a job at a big collection agency, which, as he put it, liked to "hire life's undesirables." He explained, "They tell you, 'You know what type of records you got, and you know ain't nobody else going to hire you, so you shut the fuck up.'" Jimmy hated his work environment, but he was making more than $90,000 a year, which helped him support his five children; and he was determined not to go back to jail. He had a young set of twins, a boy and a girl; another son; and two daughters in their teens. Jimmy was raising the twins on his own, because their mother was serving a four-year sentence in jail, though Jimmy refused to tell me why. "Man, I was Mr. Mom," he recalled. "I'm breaking down crying, ironing these little-bitty-ass pants at five o'clock in the morning, trying to get these kids ready for school. Like, man, if you let them oversleep they going to have a rough day, man. You got to get them *up.* That was worse than any street situation I was in, but the reward was so good, man."

Jimmy encouraged his older son to excel at school and go to college. But the boy didn't listen to him. One day, when he was eighteen, he justified his poor grades by announcing that he would be content to work at McDonald's. "I was hurt more than anything else when he said that," Jimmy said. "I turned around and walked away. He was like, 'Dad, you don't know what it's like out here, man.'"

Jimmy was enraged by his son's suggestion that he didn't understand the realities of life in the ghetto. He felt that his son had lost respect for him because he was working a nine-to-five office job at the agency instead of "wearing a chain" and "standing up on the corner." Jimmy said, "I lost it, dude. My son, mind you, is six-two, three hundred and twenty-five pounds. You understand what I'm saying? I picked up a crutch—there was an aluminum crutch around here—and I beat his ass." Jimmy said that it wasn't a severe beating; he didn't "bust him in his head," and his son wasn't bleeding. After this incident, the police came and arrested Jimmy and put him in jail for three days. When Jimmy's bosses at the collection agency learned of his arrest, they fired him.

It was at this moment, in early 2008, that Jimmy started working for Bill, managing a handful of collectors. The agency made no attempt to hide its aggressive approach to collections; its website even had a section entitled "Why Use a Collection Agency" that made one of the industry's oft-repeated boasts: "Debtors will often pay a collection agency even though they never cooperated with the original creditor, mainly because collection agencies typically increase the psychological anxiety associated with a debt."

Jimmy claims that he was both a manager and the agency's top collector. He also claims he was supposed to get 30 percent of the shop's profits at the year's end but never saw much of the money that he was due and that Bill effectively "robbed" him. Bill denies that they ever had a partnership—formal or informal—and adds that Jimmy was a mediocre collector who was lucky to be making his wage of $26 an hour. It's impossible to know exactly what their arrangement was. They had no written contract. In early 2009, a woman filed a lawsuit against Bill's collection agency; she named Jimmy as a defendant and she submitted a letter from Bill's agency, on company letterhead, listing Jimmy as a "senior partner." Whatever the nature of their professional relationship, when they parted ways in 2009, Jimmy clearly felt cheated and was determined to become his own boss.

My driving tour with Jimmy came to an end when we reached a sprawling factory complex that had been converted into a series of offices. This was where Bill's agency had been located, before Bill shut it down for good in October 2011. The hallways were eerily vacant, and the only person we encountered was an artist locking up his studio. Jimmy paused for a moment by a window near the entranceway to the suite where Bill's shop once operated. Jimmy recalled that he and Bill used to look out this window together and take in the view—a beleaguered landscape of dilapidated houses. "We used to talk about how we want to build [up] an office, and what we was willing to do to get the fuck up out of here."

After parting ways with Bill, Jimmy opened his own agency in July 2009. He took what he had learned at Bill's shop and, to a great extent, replicated it at his own agency. Jimmy's operation was, in many ways, a typical one for the impoverished East Side of Buffalo. When I first visited, in 2010, it was situated in a former karate academy, and just inside the entrance there was a long check-in counter, of the type found at any run-of-the-mill gym. Mirrors still lined the walls, and marooned exercise equipment cluttered the space. Vinny, a lean twenty-six-year-old with a heavy five o'clock shadow, sat behind the check-in counter. He was the only white employee, and was second in command at the office, though Jimmy occasionally complained about his immaturity. Vinny liked to goof off, and, as Jimmy put it, "holler at broads, which is cool, because I was probably doing the same thing when I was his age." Jimmy went on, "But it's hard to have a corporate structure, man, when you don't have a corporate structure."

Jimmy's point callers were all stationed in a back room. They were mainly young African-American men in their twenties. One of them was a twenty-four-year-old former crack dealer named Jamal. "I really do want to live a law-abiding life," he told me. "I got a wife and two sons—I am trying to live for them." Jamal told me that Jimmy was his inspiration: "I always watched

Jimmy as a young boy doing the wrong thing, and now I am watching him as an adult do the right thing, and I'm still trying to follow his lead."

One morning, a twenty-year-old named C.J., dressed in jeans and a tank top, walked into Jimmy's office and asked for a job. It was the third time that C.J. had applied. Jimmy paid his employees a base salary of $7 to $15 an hour plus a commission. This prospect enticed C.J. "I see a couple dudes working here, and they are getting their money," C.J. explained. "I'm trying to get some money, too. I got a mouthpiece on me, you know what I mean?" I asked C.J. if he had any other job opportunities. "Hell, no!" he said.

Jimmy told C.J. that in order to be hired he would need to learn to talk the way he did "when you were in trouble with the principal at school." C.J. nodded. Afterward, Jimmy told me, "The lessons that I'm going to give him when he do come in here is not only going to help his little twenty-year-old ass in here, it's going to help him in life."

Part of what Jimmy's young employees liked about him was that even though he worked in an office, they saw him as tough. "Jimmy was never the kind of person you fucked with, and he still ain't," Jamal explained. "Don't take his kindness for weakness. The street shit is always gonna be in you."

When he made a new hire, Jimmy tutored him in the art of debt collection. He usually explained it this way: "You give a fiend five dimes and they don't pay you for them? How you going to feel?" The standard reply, Jimmy said, was "Oh, man, I'm going in that motherfucker's house, I'm blowing their phone up [i.e., call them continuously]." The career collector must be less emotional. "You can't take it personally," Jimmy said. When his point callers got frustrated by debtors who refused to pay, he offered them this analogy: "When you buy a pound of weed, you know the seeds and the sticks in the weed? You paid for that, right? Well, every account we're not going to collect. So don't get discouraged . . . The buds are the people that *want* to pay you—that's what you need to focus on."

The point callers' job was simply to find the debtor, get him on the phone, and then transfer the call to either Vinny or Jimmy. Jimmy explained, "I can sound a little bit intelligent, or what you would call 'white,' on the phone. It would take you a minute to catch on that I'm black." He gestured to the point callers, all of whom were black, and said that they generally couldn't do that. (Vinny, for his part, sounds like a cast member of *Jersey Shore*.)

"If a nigger call your house, the first thing you're going to think is he's trying to steal something," Jimmy said. "Because that's the stigmatism for black people. *I don't trust this mother-fucker—he don't sound like me.*" Jimmy said that most of his debtors were white, but that even black debtors are more likely to trust a white collector. As Jimmy put it, Vinny had "the complexion for the connection." The point callers, Jimmy noted, worked on commission, which meant that they got paid only if Jimmy or Vinny succeeded in the talk-off and persuaded the debtor to pay up.

One afternoon, Jimmy had a talk-off with a woman who had taken out a payday loan for $300. Jimmy would rather not work these types of loans. He would rather buy higher-quality paper—the kind whose debtors have jobs and permanent addresses—but banks and credit-card companies usually won't deal with operators like him. "I'll never get hold of that type of paper," Jimmy told me.

During his talk-off with the payday debtor, Jimmy confirmed the details of the loan and said brusquely, "You never paid it back."

"You don't need to give me an attitude, okay?" the woman said. "I'm trying to figure out what this is, okay?"

"Ma'am, you know what it is," Jimmy said. "It's a payday loan."

The argument escalated, and eventually Jimmy told her, "Our next call is going to be your sister." (The sister's name had been listed on the paperwork for the loan.)

The woman became more upset. "No, no, no, no," she said. "Are you going to listen to me?"

"This is a refusal," Jimmy continued, talking over the woman's voice. "You don't want to pay your bill. This is going to be considered first substantive contact. We're going to contact your sister and forward this as a refusal. We gave you an opportunity to pay it, and you didn't want to take advantage of that. We wish you . . ."

"Listen to what I am telling you!" the woman demanded.

"Best of luck, ma'am," Jimmy said, and hung up. He explained his strategy. "If I'm sitting here begging for money or begging for her to pay this bill, it puts a chink in my armor. If I hang up on you, like I don't want anything from you, nine times out of ten—especially a woman—they going to call back, because a woman don't like to be hung up on. Period."

Moments later, the woman called back.

Vinny took the call and tried to calm her down. "Ma'am, you never spoke to me, okay? Can you stop using profanity? You're on a recorder line. Please, act professional."

"I'm trying to get information on this shit, and you hang up on me?" the woman said. "*That's* very professional?"

Vinny said, "This is a litigation claim pending, ma'am. Attorneys and investors bought your debt. Okay, we're only trying to offer you an out-of-court settlement. Very simple."

"I understand," the woman said.

Vinny hit the mute button and declared, with a grin, "I'm the good guy now. Love it." Turning off the mute, he explained to the woman that although she had borrowed only $300, her current balance—with interest and late charges—was $747. "And that's without any court costs if it goes into litigation." Then he made his offer: "You can settle for three hundred, and it's going to show you paid it in full on your credit reports."

The woman thought it over, then said that she didn't have the money. Vinny ended the call. Jimmy was frustrated, but said that he'd call her again. "We might still have her," he said. "Because if she does have any care in the world for her credit, and if she has any morals, she's going to want to pay this." Incidentally, if and when this woman ever did pay, the onus would be on her to request a letter of payment from Jimmy's agency and then send it to the three major credit bureaus. Some large agencies will communicate directly with the credit bureaus, but smaller operations working older paper—like Jimmy's shop—rarely do.

Eventually, I told Jimmy about Theresa and Joanna. I described how someone had informed them that they were about to be taken to court and—in Joanna's case—arrested.

Jimmy didn't seem the least bit surprised. "That's the Buffalo Talk-Off," he told me matter-of-factly. It was illegal, he said, but common. "You hear that at the small places. Larger agencies, they fire people for talking like that because it will start going viral." Once one collector starts using this talk-off—and making more money with it—others will soon follow, he explained. Jimmy claimed that collectors usually used this "sterner" talk-off with older debt that was harder to collect on. The only problem with the Buffalo Talk-Off, said Jimmy, was that it "burned" the paper and made it difficult to resell. In fact, many buyers were leery of purchasing any paper that had been worked in Buffalo, fearing that it would be impossible to collect on it after Buffalo collectors had hounded the debtors.

I asked Jimmy if he ever used the Buffalo Talk-Off.

"We used a variation," he told me. "The 'jail' shit is what they come down on you for. Guys use that as a last resort, with old debt, to get it settled out. But that talk-off makes it hot. I would never use the 'jail' line. I say, 'This call is in reference to a prelegal matter, and we will file a judgment against you. Please call before we have to take this as a refusal.'"

"Is it true?"

"It is not true at all," Jimmy replied. "Unless you have an attorney and you are actually ready to sue." Vinny had apparently used a variation of Jimmy's talk-off—both versions were bluffs and could be considered violations of the Fair Debt Collection Practices Act, which says that "a debt collector may not use any false, deceptive, or misleading representation or means in connection with the collection of any debt."

According to the annual reports filed by the FTC, the number of complaints about "false threats of lawsuits" from collectors more than doubled between 2008 and 2012; in other words, the Buffalo Talk-Off has become increasingly prevalent. What's more, the combined number of complaints about "threats of violence" and "false threats of arrest or seizure of property" more than tripled.

When I visited the FTC's headquarters in Washington, D.C., I met with David Torok, who oversees the commission's complaint database. I asked him what explained the recent spike in reports of egregious tactics. Torok said it was impossible to say for certain, but then he speculated that there are "more consumers truly on the edge," and therefore collectors are simply "trying to squeeze even harder to get some money out of an extraordinarily dwindling pot."

I eventually asked Jimmy whether someone at Bill's office might have been using the Buffalo Talk-Off, and threatening debtors with arrest. "Yes, that is very easy to believe," said Jimmy. "A lot of people do that, especially if the owner is not around. You say whatever you can to get the money." (I found evidence of this elsewhere as well. In one lawsuit against Bill's agency, a debtor alleged being threatened with "arrest" if she didn't pay up and claimed that such harassment had caused her "mental anguish, fright, headaches, [and] insomnia.") Jimmy insisted that he never threatened debtors with the prospect of arrest or jail time—both because it was too risky and because it violated his sense of what was honorable.

Jimmy relied on his own code when interacting with debtors. He believed in collecting aggressively, but never threatening people or unnecessarily bullying them. He loathed a notorious local criminal, Tobias "Bags of Money" Boyland, who had recently been arrested and jailed on gun charges. Tobias, or "Toby" as he was known, allegedly coerced consumers into paying debts—which had often been artificially inflated—by threatening to have them arrested and their children turned over to social service agencies. And there were others like Toby. Jimmy despised this behavior. He despised Toby in particular, which was awkward because they had the same barber. "Every time I seen him walking in the barbershop, man, I left," Jimmy said. "I couldn't even stomach looking at this boy, with his Harley-Davidsons and ten-thousand-dollar belt buckles and stuff."

"We are professional nags, not con men," Jimmy said. There was, quite clearly, a ladder of honor and propriety among collectors. Brandon, for example, might hound a debtor very aggressively, but he would never buy paper of dubious origin or double-sell a file, because this was the practice of the "sharks" and "scumbags" he scorned. Jimmy, meanwhile, might buy paper without asking any questions and he might lead debtors to believe that he was about to sue them, but he would never threaten them with jail time, because this would make him a thug like Toby. For his part, Toby would, apparently, use whatever coercive means he could to collect. Each collector clung to his code and looked down on those below him with no small measure of moral superiority.

This was certainly the case for Jimmy. As he saw it, Toby made it harder to collect, because many debtors assumed that collectors were affiliated with Toby or someone like him. "You know, every time I seen this man I looked at him like, *Man, you taking food out of my kids' mouths,*" he said. "That shit ruined it."

Another reason that Jimmy hated Tobias Boyland so much was that he had drawn the attention of the state law enforcement officials. As he put it, "New York State got a hard-on for collections agencies because of brothers like Tobias." Much of the policing of debt collectors is done on the state level, by state attorneys general. It falls upon them to monitor all the thousands of smaller outfits that the FTC and CFB tend to overlook. Among these state attorneys general, New York's is a leader. Eric Schneiderman and his predecessor, Andrew Cuomo, both earned great fanfare for going after scofflaw collectors, many of whom hailed from Buffalo. In 2009, Cuomo filed a lawsuit against a company known as the Benning-Smith Group, which was made up of thirteen separate collection agencies. Workers at these agencies allegedly threatened to arrest, and even physically harm, consumers who did not pay up. According to Cuomo's office, one Benning-Smith collector "kept repeating the name of a consumer's daughter, describing various sexual things he would do to her unless the debt was paid." In 2013, Schneiderman made head-lines for shutting down an outfit known as International Arbitration Services (IAS) for lying to and intimidating consumers.

I was curious to learn more about the efforts of the New York State Office of the Attorney General—and so I interviewed all of the full-time staff members in the Buffalo bureau. There were two. I found this somewhat surprising, given that Buffalo is often called the capital of the debt-collection world. It seemed rather miraculous that this office of two could be as effective as it was, especially since its staff, by its own reckoning, was able to devote only roughly 65 percent of its time to collection-related cases. Karen Davis, who was the office's "senior consumer fraud representative," told me that, each year, she receives thousands of written complaints about debt collectors. After sifting through these complaints and investigating many of them, she singles out those companies whose alleged behavior is the most egregious, nasty, and violent. She puts those companies on her list of the worst offenders that she, personally, has to monitor. When we spoke, in the spring of 2013, there were 324 companies on her list.

One of Karen's most recent coups was the IAS case. The agency's collectors had been posing as law enforcement officers and threatening debtors with arrest. Rogue agencies, such as IAS, use fake addresses, P.O. boxes, and rented phone numbers to mask their whereabouts. As a result, a reliable address was the "golden information" that she often needed in order to shut down an agency on the list. In this particular case, Davis believed that the company was located somewhere in Canada, but she couldn't determine where exactly. "It went on for months, with us being frustrated, but we could get nowhere," Davis told me. "We just simply couldn't figure out where they were."

Then came the big breakthrough.

One day, an informant showed up at the Buffalo bureau and announced that he worked as a collector for IAS. He said he was unhappy because he had been cheated out of his pay—so unhappy that he had walked over to complain in person. *Walked.* That single word left Karen flabbergasted. "What do you mean?" she said. "They're not located in Canada?" No, said the informant, explaining that the IAS office was located just a few blocks away. Two days later, she served IAS with a subpoena. Davis's office ultimately forced IAS to shut down and assessed the owner with $10,000 in fines. And this is how a list of 325 companies was shortened to 324.

There was always the worry that a company like IAS might reopen somewhere else under a different name. According to Davis, many agency owners were relocating to Georgia because "they believe that consumer enforcement in Georgia is not as tough." If this happened, there was nothing that Davis or her office could do.

One afternoon, after I had spent the entire morning at his offices, I asked Jimmy bluntly whether he had been working stolen debt during his time with Bill. He said he didn't know the details of where or how Bill bought his paper, but that he was under the impression that Bill was buying paper properly, and that a collector usually knows when he is working stolen debt or debt that has been double-sold. In such cases, Jimmy said, debtors usually make a fuss, complaining that they have either already paid off this particular debt or that another agency just called them about it. This wasn't happening at Bill's agency with great regularity. Nonetheless, Jimmy took it as a given that at least some of the paper in the office didn't have a proper chain of title.

As it turned out, Jimmy wasn't even fully informed about

the kind of paper that he was working at his own shop. This became apparent to me when Jimmy's supplier, Larry, told me the following story. While working as a broker, Larry once had a buyer who circumvented him and made a deal without giving him the commission that he was due. In retribution, Larry hired a hacker from China to break into the buyer's e-mail account and obtain his password. Once he had the buyer's password, Larry had access to his paper. Larry then simply took a portfolio and subsequently sold it to Jimmy—who didn't know and didn't ask where it came from.

According to Jimmy, it was a common practice among many small agencies in Buffalo to work a few stolen or double-sold files along with the legitimate ones. They were cheaper to buy and so, he explained, "you make ends meet off the stolen shit." Working a few stolen files was just like adding "the cut," or the filler, in a package of cocaine; and it was how you padded your profit margin. With cocaine, the cut is typically baking soda, Jimmy said. "You mix it in, you put it on ice, you cool it up, man, you cool it down, that shit get hard. One turn into two. That shit—that's the dope game all the way around, man. You stretch that shit so you can make more profit."

In Jimmy's view—much like Brandon's—the economic models for selling debt and selling illegal drugs were strikingly similar. "You got the guys at the top—the hedge fund tycoons—and they are just like the big drug cartels," he explained. "They buy huge amounts of debt, and they break it up into smaller packages and sell it to dealers who then break it up again and resell it to even smaller dealers. And this continues until it hits the street level, where guys like me do the actual work of collecting. It's just like drugs, man. It's a hustle—only it's a legal hustle. That's why guys on the street, like me, we call debt the 'white man's dope.'"

Finding stolen debt was pretty easy, insisted Jimmy. You could buy it from a broker, like Larry, on the implicit understanding that it might be stolen. There were also ways to steal a file by "unmasking" it. Sellers typically sent prospective buyers a "masked" file—which meant that they had altered, removed, or blacked out certain fields in a spreadsheet, such as first names or the last four digits of debtors' social security numbers. The idea was that the prospective buyer could study the paper and try to assess its worth, but would not have the ability to collect on it until the seller sent over an unmasked version of the file. Some rogue agencies, however, were adept at covertly unmasking a file without ever paying for it. If you had a debtor's last name, for example, you could use the program called Insight to locate his social security number. Insight doesn't provide a debtor's home address, but another program called Accurint does. In this fashion, Jimmy said, it was sometimes possible to treat the masked file like a "jigsaw puzzle" and "put the file back together as if the mask wasn't there."

I subsequently got a tutorial in just how easy it could be to do this from David Hadley, an employee of a debt-brokering firm called International Credit Services in California. He was responsible for protecting the firm's files and masking them properly. David told me that sometimes sellers thought they'd removed a column from a spreadsheet—for example, a column containing debtors' social security numbers—only to have a prospective buyer access the column and use it. (This can happen, for example, when a seller uses the spreadsheet's "hide" option instead of hitting "delete.") Other times, "they replace certain letters and numbers," explained Hadley. "So people are able to rebuild it, based on, *Okay, every time I see a dollar sign that means that it is really a four. And every time I see an asterisk, that is really a six.* So the sellers think they are being good about masking it up, but they are using a similar tactic every time."

Jimmy made it clear that, in his own shop at least, he was determined to operate within the law. He emphasized that he had borrowed money from his siblings to start this venture—that he had struggled his entire life to be in control of his own fate—and he didn't want to tarnish his efforts. He saw his agency as a fresh start for himself, even though elements of his old life often resurfaced. Not long ago, for example, Jimmy hired an old acquaintance whom he knew from his time in prison. The acquaintance proved to be a lazy collector; Jimmy fired him, and the man soon reappeared in Jimmy's office brandishing a gun. Jimmy said he was often being tempted to go back to his old ways, especially as lately his agency was barely turning a profit.

Whatever the reason—whether it was the bad economy or the quality of Jimmy's paper—business had been especially slow lately. "If I let everyone know we were teetering on the edge of financial destruction, they would start jumping ship," he confided. On one afternoon that I spent with Jimmy, his point callers sent only a single call his way. "If you want to be a rogue agency, you can leave certain messages—like, 'The police are coming to get you right now'—and these phones would be ringing off the hook," Jimmy said. "But, you see, whatever messages that we are leaving are not creating a sense of urgency, because the phones are not ringing."

Jimmy said he worried that his point callers might start getting more reckless in the effort to intimidate debtors. The previous week, he had to fire a point caller, a woman. Inside her cubicle was a memo with her talking points, which included, "The call is concerning a hearing being filed in your county," and "Did you get served a summons for anything?"

The first statement was almost certainly untrue, and the second was misleading. As soon as Jimmy understood what was happening, he told the point caller, "Baby girl, this is your last day." Jimmy tolerated a certain amount of maneuvering within a gray area of the law, but she had—apparently—pushed it too far on too many occasions. Jimmy told me, "You got to separate yourself from those type of people—you got to. You know what I mean? But, for some bosses, you looking at it like, *Man, shit, this the bitch who's getting the money.*"

One afternoon, over the summer, Jimmy and I were driving around together in the Bailey-Delavan neighborhood when he caught a glimpse of someone he recognized. He slammed on the brakes and hopped out of his car. I waited by myself in the passenger's seat, puzzled and somewhat uneasy, for ten minutes or so.

Finally, he returned to the car.

"It was that dude," explained Jimmy as he got back inside. "Which dude?" I asked. It was the former employee who had pulled a gun on him, Jimmy said. He was shaking with anger. Jimmy had been unable to find him.

He started driving again. "Back when he ran up into my office with that gun, I'll tell you what, *it felt good*," said Jimmy. "My adrenaline was pumping. I wanted to shoot him." He paused, then continued. "It has been a real tear between the nigger that I *was* and the nigger that I *am*. Now, the way things are, everything has to be worked out and talked out. I am not used to that. *I wanted to kill him.*" He went silent. "I think I need to get out of this town because my past is eclipsing the present," he said finally. "Sitting behind that desk, working that job, it really ain't who I am."

At this point, his shoulders were trembling and he began to sob. "That shit ain't who I am. I am an animal. I want to do something to that nigger. As much as I hate that shit, I love it, too. I know who he is—up on that corner, selling drugs—and I don't want to be into that. I don't want them streets, but I miss them so much." Jimmy drove silently now, heading back to the office. Then, under his breath, he added, "I feel like I am living someone else's life here."

There were two things that Jimmy did to find relief—fire guns at the shooting range and go to church. One evening, I accompanied him to a midweek service. We parked in a vast lot surrounding a cavernous brick building. As Jimmy got out of his Navigator, he grabbed a small black bag, unzipped it, and pulled out a Bible. "This is my new gun," he joked. "This is where I go to blow off steam, when I got to look deep inside myself for the energy to keep going." We spent the next hour or so singing hymns and participating in Bible study. At one point, when the entire congregation was singing "Show Yourself Strong," with a choir and a band, Jimmy glanced across the aisle and saw a kid doing his homework. "This is positivity," he said.

After church, we drove around for a while, and eventually we ended up back in the parking lot behind his collection agency. Jimmy turned off the engine, sat back in his seat, and sighed.

"I got two hundred fucking dollars in the bank, and payroll is tomorrow," he told me. I asked him what he was going to do. For starters, he said, he wasn't going to be able to pay Vinny his weekly salary, which was more than a thousand dollars.

"Everything be all right," he said finally. "I think I'm just telling myself that right now because I'm in a bad fucking place, bro. I do a job that's hated by everybody and anybody on both sides of the fence, and it ain't even doing that well, man. I got people that's depending on me. My mama, my kids and shit, and even these employees, man. And every day I be just trying to think of how to keep shit afloat, bro. And wondering when they going to come knocking and shut shit down, man. You know what I mean? And I hold my head so high that people don't see the pain."

He said he didn't have to be broke. He could pick up the phone and have "ten keys"—or kilos—of cocaine in a minute. But he vowed this was something he was not going to do. Jimmy said he wasn't sure if he would even have the cash to take his kids to the movies that weekend. "They deserve to go see *Shrek* tomorrow, man," he told me. "My son has got the highest average in the fourth grade. I got good kids, man."

Though there are many lower-tier collection agencies in Buffalo, they're countered by a good number of respected agencies as well. These are the sorts of agencies that often work directly for the banks and have elaborate monitoring systems in place to make sure that their collectors follow the Fair Debt Collection Practices Act. One afternoon, I drove to Cheektowaga, just outside of Buffalo, and visited a prominent debt-collection agency called Northstar, which works on consignment for some of the nation's largest creditors.

After spending time at both Jimmy's and Brandon's small shops, I was curious to see how they compared with a big corporate agency that worked the very best paper—paper that the original creditors had not yet sold. This paper had not been "beaten up" by a long string of collection agencies. These accounts were fresh. And these debtors—or many of them, anyhow—were likely the sorts who had just started to fall behind on their bills and had not yet gone under. These were the people who might actually have some savings stashed away for an emergency. This was the kind of paper that Jimmy would never get his hands on.

The interior of the Northstar facility is lined with cubicles and looks like a typical call center, unless you happen to visit on the fifteenth of the month, as I did. At 2:00 p.m., the agency began celebrating Bonus Check Day. The lights dimmed. A disco ball began to spin, and blue, green, and red lights flashed. Noisemakers sounded; confetti was dropped. And four hundred debt collectors began to cheer. One of the agency's executives, Maggie Long, grabbed a microphone and called out to the crowd, "Are you ready for some bonus checks?"

There were hoots and whistles as Long announced the month's top ten earners, those who had collected more than $25,000 in fees that month. (Northstar says that it typically earns fees of 20 percent on collected debt.) The mood was euphoric. As one manager later described it to me, "You feel the energy running through you—it's like walking down the Strip in Las Vegas."

The top earner was twenty-seven-year-old Jason Poeller, who had collected $51,123 in fees. Long handed him a bonus check for $10,000 and the kind of boxer's belt that heavyweight champs wear. The crowd cheered. Poeller, who was delivering pizzas before he started working at Northstar three years ago, told me, "I've been hoping to do this since I first came here."

Joel Castle, Northstar's founder, was present for the ceremony, and he told Poeller, "You broke the office record."

Poeller, swallowing hard, made no reply.

"This is a record year for us in profits," Castle later told me. "Our business is up thirty-five to forty percent."

Abruptly, the overhead lights came back on, the disco ball stopped turning, and the collectors returned to their desks. As work resumed, I chatted with Lashari Huling, a thirty-eight-year-old woman who has been in collections for more than a decade, and now works as a manager at Northstar.

"This is an excellent, excellent place to work," she told me. One of the keys to success, she said, is that "you have to empathize with debtors but not have sympathy, because if you have sympathy you don't get paid." She told me that, a day earlier, she had been attempting to collect on a defaulted auto loan. The debtor was a disabled veteran who was paralyzed from the neck down. "I listened and I let him go through how he had fought for our country," Lashari recalled. "I let him vent how he didn't get the veterans' benefits that he was promised." She inquired if there was anyone who could help him. Eventually, she managed to reach the veteran's ex-wife. "I spoke with her," Lashari said. "She wanted to help him, and she transferred the debt onto a credit card that she had."

Lashari said that when she was a novice she used to get very emotional about her work. "I used to cry—oh, yeah," she told me. "It still touches home sometimes. But I have to work."

Payday at Jimmy's agency was a somber affair. That morning, he had tried to cash several postdated checks and credit-card payments provided by his debtors. They were small amounts, ranging from $100 to $250. Of the payments, $514 cleared, and another $747 bounced. Jimmy said that he hadn't earned any money the previous day. "I am fucking disgusted right now," he told me.

In the afternoon, Jimmy's point callers came by to pick up their commission checks. One of the callers, a former car salesman named Ted—Jimmy's oldest employee at fifty-eight—received $115. Another employee, Robert, made just $88.

"Now I got to go home and tell the kids, 'Okay, well, we're short on cash because Dad didn't make any money today,'" Robert told me. "I'm going to take the little money I have, and I'm going to take my kids to the zoo and enjoy the rest of the day. That's how I'm going to resolve this matter."

"Now you see why people break the law to get money in this business," Jimmy added. "That's why agencies open and close so quickly. They're either operating illegally or they can't keep up."

After his point callers were paid, Jimmy said he wanted to take a drive, and he invited me to come along. Jimmy tried to turn on the car's sound system, but it didn't work properly, and he cursed the car for being such a "hoopty." He pulled up next to a bank. The security guard, a large young man with a beard, came over to us.

"You look like me," Jimmy said, with a smile.

"*You* look like *me*," the young man replied. It was Jimmy, Jr., the son whom Jimmy had once beaten. "He only got a job because he seen me working," Jimmy had told me. "That's my reward, man."

The previous night, Jimmy had told me, "I hope that God blesses me to move on to other things—more secure things for me and my family." He wasn't sure if the agency could last much longer. "After this, bro, with my record, I'm not getting no job nowhere else. No matter how smart I am, or whatever the case may be, the only thing I'd probably be able to do is work in another collection agency—unless I work for myself. You know what I mean? This *it*, bro."

10

GEORGIA

You might think that collection shops like Jimmy's represent the last and lowest link in the food chain—the final resting place for the most beaten-up, hard-to-collect-on paper. They don't. Below the hedge fund managers, the reputable debt brokers, the midsize agencies, the mom-and-pop shops, the black-market dealers, and even the collectors like Jimmy who were just barely hanging on—below all of these players are the toughest collectors and the final stop for debt in America: the lawyers. Why the lawyers? Because they have a competitive edge—they can use the power of the courts to their advantage.

In 2009, Aaron Siegel sold 233 accounts from the Package to a company in Georgia named Associated Receivables, Inc., which promptly hired a local law firm to collect on the accounts. Making this deal was no small feat. Once a portfolio of debt has been to Buffalo, it's marked for life. If paper has been owned or collected by a Buffalo company, the assumption is that it has been beaten up, tapped out, and collected upon by any means necessary. Potential buyers simply assume the worst. Such is the city's stigma. For example, when I visited Tom Borges—the debt broker who once ran a Christian collection agency—he received a voice mail from an angry client in Buffalo: "Sell that fucking package! I'm serious. I'm fucking pissed! End of fucking story." It couldn't be helped, explained Tom. "It's not moving because it's been worked in Buffalo." And this was, often enough, Aaron's predicament as well. He was from Buffalo and even though many of the collection agencies that he hired were *not* based in Buffalo, he still had to overcome his buyers' skepticism.

When Aaron sold the 233 accounts to Associated Receivables, he did so for 1.4 cents on the dollar. This was quite a coup considering that Aaron had bought them for a penny on the dollar; done his best to collect on them; and was now selling them at a 40-percent markup. But Aaron had known what he was doing. Collection lawyers are the equivalent of relief pitchers in baseball: they only appear late in the game to make a final push. It makes no sense to introduce them earlier in the process because suing debtors is expensive; after all, there is the cost of compensating the lawyers, paying various court filing fees, and hiring someone to find a debtor's assets (if they have any). By contrast, it is much cheaper to pay a collector in Buffalo fourteen dollars an hour to make phone calls and collect money over the phone. Yet when the collectors fail, the lawyers step in.

After purchasing the accounts, Associated Receivables hired the Savannah law firm Sherwin P. Robin & Associates to collect on at least some of them. The debtors were all people who lived in Georgia and, unbeknown to them, were on the verge of falling into a legal quagmire. Their ranks included a young prison guard, a schoolteacher, a handyman who was raising two of his grandchildren, an accountant, and an immigrant from

India who had worked as a car salesman and then opened his own steakhouse. Their fortunes were now lumped together. I decided to follow these 233 accounts—which I dubbed the "Georgia Splinter"—down into the courts to see what happened at the bitter end of this trail of debt.

One debtor in the Georgia Splinter, Shelton, was a twenty-nine-year-old man who had recently moved across the border to Greenville, South Carolina, where he now worked as a prison guard. I first spoke with him over the telephone in the spring of 2013, before I headed down to Georgia. At the time, he had just discovered that his bank account had been garnished and that his next paycheck—along with any money that remained in his bank account—would be going directly to Sherwin P. Robin & Associates. This would leave him unable to pay his bills, including his car insurance, which meant that he would no longer have a reliable way of getting to work. "This whole month I will have to see how I can live by day to day and pay my bills," he told me. "Because they're taking all my money."

I met Sherwin P. Robin in Savannah, Georgia, at an old speak-easy known as the Crystal Beer Parlor. It was a cozy, dimly lit brick pub rumored to have served "hooch" throughout the Prohibition era—and the place still seemed the perfect setting for discreet conversation. We spent the better part of three hours sipping iced tea in an old-fashioned wooden booth in a corner of the pub. Sherwin was a soft-spoken middle-aged man dressed in a pink Polo button-down and a pair of white slacks. There was something decidedly old-fashioned about Sherwin, and he pined for the days earlier in his career when people in Georgia still harbored a kind of reverence for lawyers. At the courthouses, the old bailiffs would address him as

"colonel"—in tribute to the rank often bestowed upon lawyers in the old Confederate army. There was once a belief,
said Sherwin, that a lawyer was an officer of the court and
therefore entitled to some respect. "At that time, if I wrote you
a letter, people would respond, 'A lawyer wrote me. Oh, my God!
I'm in such trouble!'" Nowadays, he said, no one worried
about a letter from a lawyer reminding them about money
they owed.

Part of the problem was the banks, Sherwin said. Starting in
the 1990s, financial institutions started bombarding Georgians
with preapproved credit cards, which ultimately caused a back-
lash. Over the years, Georgians had been overexposed to debt
collectors and become "anesthetized to collection efforts," he
said. For a while, people responded to his threats only when
he sued them. "Then they started paying attention only when I
got a judgment. Today, they don't pay attention until I garnish
their wages."

Sherwin took a long sip of his drink and then confided in
me: "I hate to put it this way, but it's almost like they're glad
they're being garnished because then we're making the decision for them."

In running his own law firm, Sherwin insisted that he only
took clients who furnished him with paper that had a clean
chain of title and plenty of documentation. Most of his clients,
he said, were big national companies that hired him to sue
debtors who happened to live in Georgia. Sherwin had only
a few smaller, Georgia-based clients—including Associated Receivables, which was the entity that had purchased the Georgia
Splinter. Sherwin also told me that he generally had a high level
of confidence in the paper that he was suing on. I asked him to
what extent he could—implicitly—trust the quality of the paper
that his clients provided. Wasn't it possible, for example, that

somewhere along the way—perhaps even at the level of the original creditor—mistakes were made? "Humans make mistakes," he told me. He then added, "It does not surprise me when a creditor makes a mistake—it surprises me when the customer doesn't dispute it. If you don't, then look, it's your fault. When Washington Mutual sends out an account that was not good and the customer doesn't object, and lets it go, then that's what happens. The side that shows up wins. Not everyone gets a trophy."

As it turns out, the written contract between Aaron and Associated Receivables anticipated the possibility that there might be precisely these sorts of mistakes. It mirrored the contract Aaron had signed with Hudson & Keyse when he bought the Package: it promised almost nothing. The contract noted, "There is no representation or warranty either given or implied as to the accuracy, truthfulness or completeness of any or all information contained in Exhibit B." Exhibit B, it turns out, was the "electronic file" providing all the information about the debtors and what they owed.

And there were problems.

I tracked down a dozen or so of the 233 debtors from the Georgia Splinter and, even in this small sample, there were a number of serious issues. One woman, named Rachele, had actually paid Bill's agency (though Franklin Asset didn't know this when it sold her account). Another case involved a schoolteacher named Amy, who owed $4,271 on her Washington Mutual credit card. Before charging off this debt, Washington Mutual gave her a credit of $608, forgiving her interest on the account and reducing her balance to $3,663. Official bank records confirm this. Yet when Aaron Siegel's company purchased the account, the balance was back to $4,271. Somewhere along the way, quite possibly at the bank itself, the $608 credit had been forgotten. (This had happened to both Joanna and Theresa as well.) A difference of $608 can have big consequences when interest is factored in. Amy's debt, for example, had been charged off in July 2007. If she had to pay 29 percent interest—and many debt buyers charge that rate—this $608 would have generated an additional $1,234 in interest by July 2014. Amy was somewhat lucky in this regard. In a letter, Sherwin P. Robin & Associates told her it charged only 18 percent.

The strangest story involved a debtor named Julie, an accounting analyst, who told me that she did not recognize the debt she was being sued over. Part of the problem was that the same debt appeared on her credit report in two places, as if it were two separate debts from two separate creditors: Chase and Washington Mutual. As it turns out, Julie's original creditor was Providian, which was then bought by Washington Mutual, which was then bought by Chase. Julie was thoroughly confused. And she wasn't alone. A source at the CFPB told me that as debts are sold from one buyer to another—and interest is added along the way—consumers will often receive calls from a collection agency they've never heard of, on behalf of a creditor that they've never done business with, over a balance that they don't recognize.

I called Paul Hartwick, the head of public relations for Chase Credit Card Services, to help make sense of Julie's predicament. After conducting his own investigation, Hartwick told me that Chase was simply going to call the debt "fraud" and request that it be removed from her credit report. I was surprised and I asked him for an explanation. He gave two reasons: the first was that Julie claimed that she didn't recognize the charges on the card; the second was that Chase didn't have much of Julie's original paperwork, including her original application for the card or the subsequent records of who was actually paying the account. When I asked where the paperwork had gone, he replied, "I don't know." He then added that when Chase acquired Washington Mutual—in one of the most important financial rescues of recent times—it was "a really rapid transition." *At some point, Washington Mutual did have these records—right?* "Presumably," replied Hartwick.

"So it's anyone's guess what happened to them over time?"

"I don't know. It could be a lot of different things. It could be simply bad record keeping, it could be a systems conversion [problem], where things were not retained. It could have been a variety of different things."

Rachele, Amy, and Julie were all being asked to pay amounts that they might not have owed—or simply didn't owe. But whose responsibility was it to address that? The original creditors, who sold these debts long ago, had no motivation to intervene. Meanwhile, the lawyers like Sherwin—who are responsible for suing on such accounts—are often given limited information and have no easy way of verifying it. Consumer advocates argue that debt buyers who seek judgments based on unverified or unverifiable information are fully culpable. Whoever is to blame, these mistakes aren't freak occurrences. They are the inevitable result of a haphazard system that transfers debt from one vendor to another—over and over—with minimal oversight or incentive to get it exactly right. Ira Rheingold, who heads the National Association of Consumer Advocates, says mistakes like these occur whenever debt is bought and sold. "It's something like a game of telephone," says Rheingold. "The information is just going to get worse and worse and worse."

One morning, I traveled to Douglas County, on the outskirts of Atlanta, where I observed a session of Magistrate Court, which is Georgia's equivalent of small-claims court and—in this instance—could have been called debtors' court. Several of the debtors from the Georgia Splinter lived in Douglas County, and I was curious to see what their experiences in court might have been like. I showed up early and met a middle-aged married couple who, as it turns out, were not part of the Georgia Splinter. The husband, Frederick, told me that he was a former Marine corporal who spent seven years in the service, including a lengthy stint serving at Guantánamo. Frederick's wife, Keanne, sold shoes for a living. Keanne was actually the defendant in the case, and she appeared so wound up that she spoke to me only in short, tense replies.

Keanne was being sued over an American Express account that she had taken out in 2005. Although the card was in Keanne's name, it was mainly Frederick who had used it in order to buy supplies for his construction business. The Great Recession had hit Frederick especially hard, as it had so many contractors in the Atlanta area. "It was like one day, the water is flowing through the stream, and then it just stopped," Frederick told me. "All of a sudden, the banks stopped the lines of credit for buyers, and you're just stuck." At the time, Frederick had just purchased two new properties and renovated them. He had buyers lined up and the buyers had mortgages lined up. "Then the banks backed out on the buyers for their mortgages. I had to let the houses go. I couldn't pay the contractors. And I owed the credit-card bill for the supplies." The burden of all of this fell on Keanne. She had, or at least used to have, good credit—better than Frederick, anyhow—and that's why they had taken out the American Express card in her name. Now it was Keanne, not Frederick, who had to stand up before the judge and explain the situation. It was a prospect that clearly terrified her. To further complicate matters, she did not recognize the name of the debt buyer that was suing her or know how, if at all, it was connected to American Express.

Before court was called into session, a young man in a suit walked into the atrium and called out Keanne's name. He explained that he represented the debt buyer and he wanted to speak with us. Frederick and Keanne introduced themselves and I explained that I was an author, observing the courts.

"I'm not comfortable with you being here," said the lawyer.

"We *are* comfortable with him being here," Frederick said.

The lawyer hesitated as if reluctant to proceed. He eventually handed Frederick and Keanne a bill for $3,762 that looked like a credit-card statement, only in two separate places it stated: "This is an account summary. It is not a credit card statement from the originating creditor and has not previously been provided to the consumer." It was hard to know what, exactly, this document was. It looked as if someone might have transposed information from a spreadsheet—including a name, an address, dates, an account number, and a balance—and used it to create a mockup of a credit-card bill. There was no detailed listing of purchases, payments, or fees and it was impossible for Frederick to know, at a glance, whether the amount of $3,762 was accurate. Frederick asked the lawyer if he had any of the original paperwork, including the original signed contract. The lawyer replied that, under Georgia case law, he was not required to provide the original signed contract. I chimed in and pressed the lawyer on whether he actually had this or any of the other original paperwork. I was genuinely curious.

"Are you an attorney?" the lawyer asked me.

"No," I told him.

The lawyer then said he would have to talk to the judge because I was not allowed to "represent" them.

"He's not representing us," protested Frederick.

This conversation continued for the next several minutes, with Frederick again asking for more paperwork, so that he could understand the nature of the $3,762 that they owed and whom, exactly, they owed it to. The lawyer finally told Frederick and Keanne, "Let's take it in front of the judge."

We all proceeded into the courtroom. Moments later, the lawyer tapped me on the shoulder and gestured for me to follow him back outside. He said he intended to have *me* sworn in and brought before the judge as a witness. I thought he was joking until, several minutes later, the judge gestured for me to stand next to Keanne, raise my right hand, and promise to tell the truth, the whole truth, and nothing but the truth. The young lawyer, who was suing Keanne, then began with his opening arguments—namely that I was representing the defendant and was thus practicing law without a license. He then asked the judge to instruct me that I could face "criminal sanctions" for doing this.

I felt that I should say something in my own defense because I was, apparently, on trial at this point. I recounted what had happened, explaining that I had introduced myself as an author and had merely asked one or two simple questions during this pretrial meeting. No one, I argued, could possibly infer that I was playing lawyer and mounting a vigorous defense.

The judge nodded her head thoughtfully.

The young lawyer, still looking quite determined, then asked the judge to instruct me that I could not write about what I had witnessed earlier because it was all confidential. The judge apparently agreed because she then turned to me and explained, "You can't put any of that in your book." I waited for a more detailed explanation of why, but none was offered. Throughout all of this, Keanne stood alongside me, quietly waiting her turn to participate in a lawsuit that concerned the $3,762 that she allegedly owed. Finally, the judge asked the lawyer what he wanted to do over the matter of the debt. The lawyer asked for a moment to consult with his client by phone. He stepped out of the courtroom and then, moments later, returned and said that he would be dismissing the case.

After leaving the courtroom, both Keanne and I were thoroughly confused. I knew from experience that the presence of a journalist or author could ruffle or unnerve some people, but that alone couldn't explain what had just happened. And what, exactly, had just happened? Frederick and Keanne had shown up in court, along with me, and we had asked the lawyer to provide the evidence that supported his case. Little did we realize that this simple action *was* the equivalent of mounting a vigorous defense.

Later, I got to talking with a lawyer named Michael Tafelski, who worked for Georgia Legal Services, representing poor debtors. Tafelski had been in court that morning and had witnessed much of what had transpired. He told me he wasn't in the least bit surprised that the case had been dismissed. In order to prevail in cases like this one, all a debtor had to do was show up and utter the "magic words."

"What are the magic words?" I asked.

"Prove your case," replied Tafelski, meaning present some evidence.

According to Tafelski, creditors' lawyers almost never had enough evidence to withstand careful scrutiny or cross-examination in court. And so they tried to corner debtors in pretrial and get them to sign a "consent agreement," a legal document admitting that they owed the money and promised to pay it. This was what I had witnessed and unwittingly interrupted. And the strategy worked most of the time, Tafelski said. Most debtors simply never showed up in the first place, he explained, and those who did often signed the consent agreement. For those debtors who were nervous—and perhaps had never been to a courthouse before—signing on the dotted line and avoiding an encounter with a judge might seem like a good idea.

At another Georgia courthouse, I met a defendant named Gwen, who was being sued by a company called Midland Funding LLC. Midland was, it seemed, the owner of a number of unpaid Target credit-card accounts, including Gwen's. Gwen showed up ten minutes late to court, protesting the debt. At this point, the judge had already marked her as a no-show and had entered a default judgment against her. After apologizing profusely, Gwen begged the judge to reconsider her situation. Gwen had actually already made her case in writing, in papers that she had submitted to the court a month earlier. She had written: "This account was already disputed and found to not be my account. This dispute was won against Target National Bank in January 2012. The account per Target was then removed from my records and credit history." After reviewing her papers, the judge was apparently persuaded, because he voided the default judgment and allowed the hearing to go forward. At this point, the lawyer for Midland Funding immediately dismissed the case. The whole scenario seemed to play out exactly as Michael Tafelski had described. A debtor showed up, pushed back, and the case was dropped. In this case, there was the added possibility that the debt might not even have been Gwen's.

In truth, Gwen and Keanne were the outliers—because they actually showed up in the courtroom. The vast majority of debtors, roughly 90 percent by most estimates, are no-shows.

That fact struck me as rather astounding. *How was it that nine out of ten people simply didn't appear in court to defend themselves?* It seemed possible that many of them had become "anesthetized" to calls from collectors, as Sherwin Robin put it. Many debtors don't understand that if they fail to respond to a legal complaint or show up in court to contest it, they are effectively opening up their bank accounts to being garnished. It may also be that they're not able to pay the debt, and so contesting it seems pointless. Sometimes the fault lies with the "process servers" who are hired to hand-deliver the notices to debtors informing them that they are being sued. In a phenomenon sometimes called "sewer service," process servers never deliver the papers they are given, but then file a false affidavit saying that they did. (In 2009, the New York State attorney general brought a lawsuit against several law firms and collection agencies for sewer service, alleging that 100,000 consumers had been victimized and that over $500 million had been seized improperly.) Another explanation is that the debtors do show up at court, but never enter the courtroom because they meet with a lawyer in pretrial and sign the "consent agreement," promising to pay. This is what Frederick and Keanne almost did.

Whatever the explanation, debtors rarely go before an actual judge. And this simple reality shapes the entire market for debt. John H. Bedard, Jr., a Georgia-based lawyer who represents and advises creditors' lawyers, made this very point when I met him, several days later. In Bedard's frank and thoughtful account, the high default rate shapes the entire industry—everything from the price of debt to the evidence that collection attorneys bring to court. "When no one shows up, the plaintiffs are not generally required to put up their evidence," he explained. This meant that the debt buyers had no incentive to obtain the kind of documentation that would hold up in court as admissible evidence—documentation proving that "the debt exists and the person whom you've sued owes it."

The absence of such documentation is striking. In 2013, an FTC study found that six of the nation's largest debt buyers typically receive very few documents at the time of purchase. When purchasing debts, the FTC noted, these buyers received the "account statements"—that is, the actual monthly bills where charges appear, with dates, on an item-by-item basis—for just 6 percent of the accounts that they purchased. And the debt buyers received copies of the original account applications—the documents proving that consumers opened the account and agreed to the terms—for less than 1 percent of accounts that they purchased. What's more, debt buyers often did not receive a breakdown of what debtors owed in principal, interest, and fees.

In Bedard's view, the original creditors were only willing to sell debt cheaply—for pennies on the dollar—so long as they were *not* asked to delve back into their records and find more information or evidence. Retrieving such information often proved labor-intensive and costly. If the banks had to do this, the result would be a higher price for the same debt. Meanwhile, the debt buyers weren't interested in paying more for this additional documentation, because they usually didn't need it. As Bedard saw it, everything hinged upon consumers' not showing up in court to contest the evidence—or the lack thereof. He maintained that if all the debtors in America started showing up in court, the effect would be colossal. "It would bring the debt-buying industry, as we know it, to a grinding halt," Bedard told me.

Some debt buyers do go through the trouble of obtaining records—typically affidavits from the banks—so that they'll have compelling evidence when they sue debtors in court. Even then, there's a problem: not all banks are able to furnish accurate records. There have been numerous reports, for example, that Chase—the nation's largest bank—was simply "robo-signing" affidavits en masse with little regard for accuracy. Mac McGinn, who ran Chase's "media research department," explained to me how the process worked. Before bringing a lawsuit, a debt buyer would ask Chase to verify the exact amount of money a debtor owed. They would then send Chase an unsigned affidavit to be reviewed and signed. Those unsigned affidavits would come to McGinn, whose department handled all queries about old paperwork. He would ask the bank's notaries, who worked for him, to sit down with a Chase bank officer. That officer would—in theory—review each individual request carefully and then sign an affidavit. Often, says Mac, the bank officers would sign two hundred to three hundred affidavits in a little over an hour. Sometimes the bank officer doing the job would have little to no experience reviewing these types of records. According to Mac, they were just signing whatever was placed in front of them. "There's no way in hell that you could go through that many affidavits and not have some sort of error," he told me. The bank allowed it, he said, because it was able to charge for each and every affidavit it provided: "The bank was making money, they didn't care what was going on." When I asked him for his reaction, he told me, "I was pissed at what they were doing."

At one point, Mac raised his concerns with a superior. Mac said that she, and the other "higher-ups," were unconcerned, so he "let it go." Mac left Chase in 2008. Chase has never admitted to any wrongdoing—though in 2013, the Office of the Comptroller of the Currency ordered the bank to improve its legal debt-collection practices and ensure that its affidavits were, in fact, accurate. Chase then announced that it had ceased all of its own efforts to sue its former customers over credit-card debts.

Down in Georgia, creditors were often suing debtors en masse under similarly troubling circumstances. At one point, I spoke with a Georgia lawyer named Dennis Henry, who used to work for one of the biggest collection law firms in the state. He was in charge of all the outgoing legal paperwork. Henry said that his firm was filing roughly ten thousand new lawsuits against Georgia debtors each month. Dennis's job was to sign the paperwork on every single one of these lawsuits. The Fair Debt Collection Practices Act prohibits debt collectors, including lawyers, from making false representations. When a letter is sent on a lawyer's letterhead, for example, a debtor is likely to assume that the lawyer is actually involved in the process and—consequently—that this is a very serious matter. In situations like this, courts have said that the lawyer must be "meaningfully involved" in the process. That's where Dennis came in. He was to review and sign every single lawsuit that the firm filed. He claims that he worked twelve-to-fourteen-hour shifts and signed roughly five hundred lawsuits a day. In theory, he was providing his lawyer's eye and making sure that everything was exactly as it should be. But it proved impossible. "There's no way that you could effectively double-check all that stuff," he told me. "No possible way." One could argue that Dennis met his obligation to be "meaningfully involved" simply by monitoring his staff (of nonlawyers) and ensuring that they understood and followed all of the requirements of the law—which is presumably the argument that Dennis would have made in court, if challenged. Only it never came to that. In the end, Dennis was fired from the firm in 2011, after a local news station produced evidence that someone else in the office might have been signing his name on legal documents as well.

Dennis admitted to me that this was true and that the person signing his name was one of his subordinates. He maintains that the firm had put him in an impossible situation. For its part, the firm said only that it disputes these facts but declined to comment in detail.

When I asked Dennis about the size of the profits that his old firm made, he offered only one word: *astronomical.*

The state of Georgia was conceived largely as a philanthropic effort to give debtors a second chance. The venture was championed by a British aristocrat named James Oglethorpe, who, in 1732, founded a colony in the New World that would—in theory—allow debtors to opt out of debtors' prison and, instead, have a fresh start as farmers. As it turns out, Oglethorpe's vision for the colony never really took hold and no significant numbers of debtors ever came from prison to the New World. And yet the myth endures that Georgia was once a place devoted to the redemption of the indebted. I wondered why and eventually posed this question to Stan Deaton, a senior historian at the Georgia Historical Society. "It's obviously not what happened, but what we wished had happened or what we like to tell ourselves happened, because it's a part of the national narrative," he told me. After all, noted Deaton, Americans yearned to believe that with hard work and pluck anyone could pull themselves out of financial ruin and reinvent themselves.

The hard truth is that such reinvention was always difficult, and may be more difficult today than at almost any other time in our recent history. Creditors often lament how easy it is for debtors to declare bankruptcy and avoid paying their debts. There is, however, another side to this narrative. There are countless

Americans with poor credit scores who are forced to live in a shadow economy, where they pay hugely inflated premiums for their cars, apartments, and loans. One of the debtors from the Georgia Splinter, a young woman named Catherine, told me that she purchased her car from a dealership in Conyers, Georgia, which catered almost exclusively to debtors. The place was called Prime Auto. I drove out to Conyers and met with one of Prime Auto's owners, Bob Weir.

When I arrived, Bob was quick to explain how his operation worked: "Well, what we can do for you is finance you an automobile at twenty-eight percent interest." Bob arranged his loans through a company called Auto Finance, which offered forty-two-month loans, with a down payment of roughly $1,000. It was Auto Finance that set the interest rates and assumed the risk that a client might not pay. Bob just sold the cars. At this very moment, he said, I could buy a 2005 Chevrolet Impala LS, with just 100,000 miles on it. It could be mine for $9,000 plus interest, which would bring my total bill, when all was said and done, to roughly $13,500. According to the NADA's *Official Used Car Guide*, this car's retail value was $7,200. I asked Bob why he was charging $9,000. It came down to credit scores, he replied. If a customer had very poor credit, Bob would have to offer the financing company an extra cash incentive—above and beyond the 28 percent that it would earn—to cement the deal. This cash incentive was known, somewhat ironically, as "the discount." A customer with bad credit might have to pay a "discount" of $1,800 in this situation, said Bob, which is why he was charging $9,000. "What it comes down to is this—if you have bad credit, your money is worth about seventy-five cents on the dollar," he explained. By the time that his clients arrived here, they didn't have that many other options. "The customer in this market is at the end of the road," he told me. Bob then corrected himself and added, "There is another road below us." Would-be clients who couldn't get financing through Bob's dealership always had the option of visiting a buy-here-pay-here lot. This was the last resort. I asked Bob where I could find such a place. "Right around the corner," he told me.

Around the corner, I found T & B Motors and its owner, Tony Scott. Tony was dressed in a bright green button-down shirt and what can only be described as khaki short-shorts, which covered no more than his uppermost thighs. Tony sat at a desk behind a sign that read, WARNING!! TRESPASSERS WILL BE SHOT. SURVIVORS WILL BE SHOT AGAIN. When I inquired about the sign, Tony pulled out a Ruger LCP .380 compact pistol. "We don't play," said Tony. "You come in here and take something that's ours, we're gonna blow a hole in you."

"Add a little ventilation," added Billy Bickers, a heavyset man with a 64-ounce mug of Coke in hand. He was one of Tony's employees.

"Pull that one out over there, Billy," said Tony.

"I try not to pull the thing out unless I want to use it," said Billy.

"Well, you might use it," said Tony, who then pointed at me. "He is a Yankee."

Billy pulled out a .357 Magnum.

The guns were a precaution, explained Tony, against any potential perpetrators—be they trespassers, robbers, or customers. Tony explained that his car dealership offered people a chance to "rebuild their credit and get back in grace with society." According to Tony, when he opened the business in the mid-1980s, his customers tended to be honest people who had fallen upon hard times. "The people that we're getting now are absolutely not trustworthy—they're nearly criminals," said Tony. The trick to dealing with them, he explained, was viewing them as "children." "If they don't behave, you have to spank 'em. You make 'em pay their payments and keep 'em straight—just like you do children." This was, apparently, how he had raised his own son. "If he didn't behave, I tore him up. Same way my daddy did me. If I didn't do right, I got my butt tore up."

"Our daddies really did it," added Billy. He then eyed his boss and added, just to clarify matters: "You're speakin' figuratively—of our customers."

"Oh yeah, I don't whip their asses," said Tony.

Tony said he had to be tough when dealing with his clientele or else he would be out of business: "The only people *they* pay are the people that make 'em pay." According to Tony, when giving out credit, some embraced "the old theory of sling the shit up on the wall and, if enough of it sticks, you'll make a living." He couldn't afford to do that, and so he had devised his own system. At T & B Motors, Tony did everything in house. He was the car dealership, the bank, the credit bureau, the collection agency, and the repo man, all wrapped up into one. Instead of choosing his customers based on their credit scores, he asked them to bring in two pay stubs proving that they were gainfully employed. He loaned them the money, set the interest rate at 24 percent, and dictated the terms for default. If they were late, Tony repossessed the car.

Tony's business model, I realized, existed at the rock bottom of the credit market. It was what existed in the complete absence of trust: a marketplace where creditors had lost faith in debtors and debtors had lost any sense of obligation—or ability—to pay. Perhaps some of this was the inevitable result of the Great Recession. For years, banks had given out credit in a freewheeling manner to virtually anyone who asked for it. Then the economy crashed and people couldn't pay their bills.

So, in the case of credit-card debt, the banks sold these debts for a few cents on the dollar and then restricted their new lending to those deemed safe bets. Yet the fact remained that all kinds of other people still needed to borrow money to purchase big-ticket items, like cars. And even with the risks involved, lenders could make money if they were tough enough and charged enough interest. This is where Tony came into the picture. With him, it was back to basics. There was a guy named Tony. He was your last resort. He charged you 24 percent interest, and, if you wanted a car, you paid it. If you didn't pay, Tony took the car. And if you caused trouble, Tony made it known that he was only too happy to whip out his Ruger LCP .380 compact pistol and add some ventilation to your shirt.

After leaving T & B Auto, I wanted to see the kind of place where Tony's customers—the worst-off debtors—might live. The Lorene Lodge in Marietta was a motel geared toward guests who wanted to have extended stays. It was located on a drab stretch of highway where storefront signs advertised bail bonds, help for drunk drivers, and cheap cars for those with bad credit. The establishment resembled a group of concrete bunkers surrounded by parking lots. A sign out front read: LORENE LODGE: WEEKLY RENTAL $130 TO $145. ALL UTILITIES & CABLE INCLUDED.

In the main office, I met the property manager, a fifty-eight-year-old man named John Carpenzano. I asked him whether many residents stayed here because their credit was too bad to live elsewhere. Yes, he replied—that pertained to "just about everybody" at the motel, including himself. As he told it, John owed his poor credit to several factors including a flood and the bad economy, which had forced him not just to work here, but live here as well. Just around the corner from the main office, I met a middle-aged woman named Joann Gaines, who invited me into her home, a cramped, dark, disheveled room with a tiny kitchenette. She told me that she was living here in large part because her credit scores were too low to live elsewhere. When I asked her whether she felt safe, she pointed toward a pan on the stove. "I gotta keep a pot of grease on," she told me.

"What do you mean?" I asked.

"If they kick your door in, and I got enough time to get up and get that grease, they'll burn up," she told me.

"They'll burn up?"

"They will burn," she confirmed. "You know what happens when something burns you. Your skin peels off. They'll think twice before going to anybody's door trying to kick it in. Grandma taught me that. She said, 'Don't kill them, just make them wish they were dead.'"

Later in the day, I had a chance meeting with a former Lorene Lodge inhabitant who had come back for a quick visit. He was a small, rotund man in his early fifties who introduced himself as Ab Smith. Ab was a recovering alcoholic and, interestingly enough, he thanked the Lorene Lodge for helping him rebuild his credit. At first, I assumed that he meant his credit score, but that wasn't it. He was speaking about "credit" in the most general sense of the word. When he first arrived at the Lorene Lodge, Ab claimed to have no "credit" at all—meaning nothing to prove that he was a dependable member of society. He was starting from scratch.

Ab gestured broadly around the grounds of the motel and declared emphatically: "This *is* scratch." He explained that when he was getting his life together and wanted a proper apartment, he needed a reference and a record that he had actually been paying his bills consistently. Ab was able to do that right here. The simple act of paying the Lorene Lodge roughly $130 to $145 a week had established a sort of de facto credit record. If anyone ever wanted to check on Ab's creditworthiness, he or she could simply call John at the front desk, and John could confirm that, yes, Ab really had paid his bills. By doing this, Ab explained, he was eventually able to move into a real one-bedroom apartment that cost him just $435 per month. A room at the Lorene Lodge, by contrast, could cost anywhere from $550 to $620 per month. For Ab, this was progress.

I took a hard look at the Lorene Lodge and saw it anew. When you lived in the shadow economy, and your credit scores were abominable or nonexistent, you didn't rely on the credit bureaus to vouch for you. You relied on a place like the Lorene Lodge. This was the starting point. Scratch. When I asked Ab if he was glad to have gotten out of the place, he looked around grimly and replied, "When I come back here, I say to myself, *This is who I don't want to be—this is not a life for a man.*"

Scratch was precisely where Shelton—one of the debtors from the Georgia Splinter—didn't want to be. Yet by the time I met him, in the summer of 2013, he was perilously close. Shelton was the twenty-nine-year-old prison guard from South Carolina whose bank account Sherwin Robin's law firm had just garnished. One morning, I drove north on the interstate, across the border into South Carolina, and met him for lunch on the outskirts of Greenville.

We met at a Ruby Tuesday alongside a strip mall. As soft rock hummed in the background and preternaturally cheerful waitresses hovered about, Shelton recounted the details of his day-to-day life. He lived in a small house with his fiancée and her mother, who was quite ill and housebound. He worked twelve-hour shifts at the local prison, and, when he came home, his phone was ringing around the clock with calls from debt collectors—so many called it was hard to keep track of them all. As a prison guard, he made just $29,000 a year. In order to enhance his take-home pay, he had opted to give up his health insurance, but that had been a mistake. He had recently gone to the hospital with chest pains and racked up a medical bill of roughly $900. The doctors said that he had high blood pressure—due, in part, to stress.

Over lunch, Shelton traced his troubles back to 2004, when Bank of America offered him a credit card with a $3,500 line of credit. At the time, he was just twenty-one years old, making close to minimum wage at a temp agency. This was back in the days of easy money when credit cards, like home mortgages, were still being given out willy-nilly. Shelton used the card to cover costs, like paying off his student loans and going out for dinner. For a year he made regular payments, usually the minimum required, and then he had a dispute over what he owed. He claims that the bank failed to record several payments that he made, and when it wouldn't adjust his balance, he stopped making payments. (Bank of America says that it has no record of him issuing a dispute or complaint over a missing payment.) Shelton is the first to admit that it was a poor choice; but, at the time, he says he didn't realize just how ill-advised and costly this decision would prove to be.

In April 2006, when Bank of America charged off his debt, he owed a principal balance of $2,464. But this was hardly all that he owed. Bank of America tacked on an additional $414 in interest and $752 in fees. Since then, Shelton's debt had only grown. In April 2010, just four years later, he received a letter from Sherwin P. Robin & Associates saying that he currently owed $8,189, but that "as a result of our difficult economic times," the firm was willing to reduce the balance. In May, he received a summons to appear in court over the matter. He never showed up to defend himself. Shelton told me that it had proven difficult to get off from work and he didn't appreciate that he was opening his wallet to pay a hugely inflated debt. In August, the State Court of Richmond County entered a default judgment against him for $5,229. By May 2013, Sherwin P. Robin & Associates had garnished $872 of his wages and was insisting that he still owed them $6,786 when factoring in interest and fees. That means, when all was said and done, Shelton was on the hook for more than *triple* his original principal balance.

In the spring of 2013, Sherwin P. Robin & Associates succeeded in garnishing Shelton's bank account, removing all of the money he had—roughly $1,000. At that point, Shelton's most pressing problem was his car. He had used a car dealership like Prime Auto that specialized in selling vehicles to people with bad credit. Just several weeks earlier, he had bought an eleven-year-old Mercedes for roughly $9,300. He put $1,500 down and agreed to pay off the remaining balance over the next forty-two months at an interest rate of 24.9 percent. That meant that, ultimately, he would be paying more than $4,000 in interest. Yet his real concern was that he would go into default, lose his car, and not be able to reach his workplace. Shelton's car actually came with a GPS feature installed that allowed his loan provider to shut off the engine, remotely, the very second that he went into default. Shelton feared that one morning soon, he would be driving to work, down a lonely country road, when all of a sudden his engine would go dead. It seemed like just a matter of time before he was stranded at the side of the road.

When lunch was over, Shelton offered to give me a tour of the area. We drove past the tiny house where he lived with his fiancée and her mother, and then we stopped briefly at the car dealership where he had purchased his car. A clerk at the dealership told him matter-of-factly that if he went into default and his car engine died, he would also lose his $1,500 down payment.

Eventually we drove to the prison where Shelton worked. It was an enormous, sprawling complex that looked a bit like a windowless shopping mall shrouded in barbed wire. We parked in the visitors' lot, situated atop a slight slope, and gazed down on the prison. I asked Shelton what kind of inmates he guarded. "Rapists, child molesters, murderers, drug dealers," he replied. He seemed lost in thought. "Soon as I pull up in the parking lot, it's like a morbid state comes over me," he told me quietly. "Like, just dreading coming to work, because you got to deal with this for twelve hours and you are locked behind these fences." Every day when he came to work, Shelton said, they scanned, frisked, and searched him. "It actually makes you feel like you are an inmate yourself."

Shelton said he worked twelve-hour shifts, without a lunch break, and it was slowly grinding him down. The worst was when he learned that his bank account had been garnished and he would take home no money for the previous two weeks of work. Shelton had no leverage to negotiate. This was because he had failed to show up in court to contest his lawsuit, forfeiting his right to challenge the amount that he owed. Hearing this story helped me understand how the system worked. Shelton wasn't blameless. Not at all. He had made some poor decisions; but in so doing, he had fallen into a trap and would have to pay dearly while his creditor, with the aid of the courts, stood to profit greatly.

So what will happen to Shelton's debt? One might think that once Sherwin Robin won a judgment against Shelton and garnished his bank account that the story would be over. But it's not. Not necessarily, anyhow. Many debt buyers actually buy and sell legal judgments. For example, Tom Borges—the debt broker from California—arranged many such deals. Tom was bullish about buying and selling judgments and, when I visited him in Napa, he explained why. We were having lunch at an upscale café when Tom pointed to a glass bottle on the table, and told me that judgments were so valuable because, once imposed, debtors were effectively trapped in the bottle: "What I mean by having the debtor in the bottle, is that you got him surrounded and captured for at least ten to twenty years. And if he goes back to work, or buys a home or sells his home, you're getting paid—as opposed to a straight-up collection account where you can't even find the guy [because] he is under the radar or he is under a rock and he has got no money. These people can't run: you already found them. You got them put on the shelf and in the bottle!" Interestingly enough, Tom told me that one of his clients was none other than Associated Receivables, which owned the Georgia Splinter. So it is possible that, at some point in the not-too-distant future, the judgment against Shelton will be crackling across the Internet, bouncing off various satellites and heading due west for Tom's offices in an immaculately restored Victorian mansion in Napa.

Astoundingly, if Shelton had only showed up in court and pressed the opposing lawyer to "prove his case"—as Michael Tafelski, had put it—the lawsuit might well have been promptly dismissed and Shelton might have owed absolutely nothing. In fact, another debtor from the Georgia Splinter, a man named Ajay, had turned this strategy into something of an art. Ajay was an immigrant from India who had a lucrative career selling cars, mainly Nissans and Toyotas. In his days as a salesman, Ajay said he lived extravagantly, "drinking, smoking, partying, and eating meat." In 2006, Ajay and his wife opened a high-end steakhouse in the suburbs of Atlanta. The place was furnished opulently, with ornate, custom-made woodwork that Ajay imported from India. To pay for this, they used their savings and a home equity loan but it wasn't enough. In the seven months that the restaurant was open, Ajay estimates that they racked up $300,000 of debt on some twenty credit cards.

Ultimately, many of Ajay's creditors sued him. Around this time, Ajay heard from a friend that he could defeat these lawsuits by making a simple request. He figured it was worth a try. So he showed up at court and told the opposing counsel, "I would like to request a sworn affidavit from the original creditor, validating the accuracy of these charges." The lawyer ultimately dropped the case. Ajay said that he had used this strategy successfully on a number of occasions. Eventually, he and his wife moved off the financial grid. They now lived entirely on cash, which they had kept on hand—just in case a creditor did obtain a judgment and came looking for their assets. "My bank account has like fifteen or twenty bucks at any given time," he told me.

When I met Ajay, in the parking lot in front of his old steakhouse, he looked as if he didn't have a care in the world. The steakhouse had since been turned into a carpet-and-flooring outlet, and he showed me around proudly—as if the place were still his. I asked Ajay if it had been stressful, slowly watching his steakhouse go broke. "I didn't lose sleep at night, because I am a very positive person," he told me cheerily.

Since then, he had stopped drinking, smoking, partying, and eating meat. He claimed that he no longer even drank tea—only water. He was, essentially, living the life of an ascetic. "I'm very happy. I have never been happier."

It was rather amazing to compare Shelton's and Ajay's vastly different fates. One of them was being held liable for three times his initial principal balance and the other seemed to have gotten off, more or less, scot-free. *What kind of system was this?* But the answer seemed clear enough. As long as 90 percent of debtors continue to do what Shelton did—not show up to question or contest their bills—it would remain a very profitable system indeed.

EPILOGUE

When he started his fund, Aaron hoped to make vast sums of money and achieve what he described as a "breathtaking level of success." By the fall of 2013, his overriding goal was simply to repay his investors and limit his exposure to the ups and downs of the collections business. At this point, Aaron had come to terms with the fact that his fund would likely lose money or break even at best. He had made some good moves, such as buying the Package; and some bad moves, such as buying the "senior citizen" paper from Bank of America. Most important, perhaps, he had launched the fund in late 2008, just before the worst of the downturn, and the economy had never really bounced back. Too many debtors had remained out of work and unable to pay their debts. This likely hurt Aaron more than anything else.

Aaron thinks often of his investors, especially John, the Texan real-estate tycoon. "I still sweat it," Aaron told me. "They've lost some money, so it's always a worry if this guy wakes up on the wrong side of the bed and decides he wants to crush me for whatever reason. I'm sure he can probably do it. I don't think that's his inclination. I don't even know what frame of mind the man's in right now. He's a very old guy. But, you know, rich old people that are cantankerous can get mad at you."

Nowadays, real estate is Aaron's main focus. Even here, however, his past has resurfaced. Not long ago, Aaron began working on a project involving the renovation of 295 apartment units. A major bank initially agreed to help finance the deal, but then balked when it learned about his history in the collections industry. Aaron was incensed, insisting that this very same bank had had no problem selling him the paper it no longer wanted. Last we spoke, he was looking to bankroll and establish what would be Buffalo's only lesbian bar. The idea came to him after he read an article in the local news about a group of gay women who periodically converged at a given bar, on a given night, and took over the place. Aaron contacted one of the organizers and proposed opening a dedicated hangout where these women could gather. "This is for profit," he told me. "But I do feel like it is my civic duty to help the city have at least one lesbian bar." Aaron was so enthused by the idea that he had called up Joseph—the Boston-based investor who had given him $1 million—and asked him if he wanted to participate. Joseph said he might be interested, though he now appeared to have troubles of his own. Just several months after our dinner in Boston, Joseph closed his hedge fund when his single largest investor withdrew its funds.

Meanwhile, to the north—in Bangor, Maine—Brandon was still entrenched in the debt business and looking to buy new types of paper. In the wake of his trip to Las Vegas, two very important deals materialized. First, he managed to buy an enormous quantity of "telco paper," some 1.8 million accounts, all of them unpaid phone bills from a host of carriers including Verizon, Sprint, and T-Mobile. The accounts had an average face value of $461 and he had bought them for just 4 basis points, or 0.04 cents on the dollar. The second deal came from the lead that he received on our trip to Las Vegas. At the time, Brandon was offered $600 million worth of older credit-card debt. In the end, he managed to buy $2 billion worth of it for 150 basis points, or 1.5 cents on the dollar. In both cases, Brandon's old friend George helped him fund the deals.

In December 2013, I paid Brandon a visit—to see how he was making out with his new paper—and was surprised to discover that his office was a veritable ghost town. His daughter, Shana, had left town; his mother had moved to Florida; and his son/brother/cousin Tony was nowhere to be seen. What's more, Brandon had let go of the vast majority of his collectors and employees, including his right-hand-man, Jeremy Mountain. When I arrived, there were just two people in the office: Brandon and Jason, the collector who had gone to jail when his gun went off (accidentally) on the public bus. Brandon was sitting at his desk, smoking a cigarette, not far from a sign that read: THIS IS A SMOKE-FREE AREA. BREATHE EASY, YOU'RE IN MAINE. Brandon quickly explained that he had shifted his business model and he was now operating primarily as a debt buyer, outsourcing the work of collecting to other agencies. He had, in effect, become Aaron.

Brandon's new business model was, apparently, both more profitable and less stressful for him. When I arrived, he was in the process of selling some of his telco paper to a woman for 25 basis points, or 0.25 cents on the dollar. Brandon himself had paid just 4 basis points, so he was making a sixfold return on his investment. "I got to mask this file and dump it over to this broad," he told me, as he typed away on his computer. This was the fifth deal that he had done with her. "She just keeps on coming back."

The industry was in flux, explained Brandon. With banks becoming so much more cautious about selling their paper, he was on the hunt for "new asset classes" like the telco paper. The Consumer Financial Protection Bureau had begun to change the game. "With the new CFPB, everyone is afraid to operate as they once did," he told me. "We are waiting for a new normal to kick in."

By early 2015, the CFPB will be issuing fairly comprehensive rules that will govern and—ostensibly—clean up the buying, selling, and collecting of debt in the United States. The fact that it has taken the federal government this long to act, however, is rather astounding. The debt-collection industry has been on the federal government's radar for some time. The FTC has issued numerous papers on the industry's problems, including an especially bleak assessment of the challenges consumers face when sued in court. In a 2010 report on the courts, the FTC concluded: "The system for resolving disputes about consumer debts is broken." Three years later, an FTC commissioner announced: "Unfortunately, since we issued our 2010 report, it appears that, in most respects, very little has changed."

Despite this, the FTC has a very modest record of enforcement. In 2009, when many Americans were being hardest hit by the economic downturn, the FTC received 88,190 complaints about debt collectors and yet the commission brought a grand total of just one "enforcement action" against a company for debt-collection violations. It brought three actions in 2010, four in 2011, six in 2012, and six in 2013. One of the six actions taken in 2013 targeted the world's largest debt collection operation, Expert Global Solutions, and carried a $3.2 million penalty. This is progress, admittedly, but it seems incremental at best. And even the CFPB's reach is limited. Its ability to enforce its much-heralded new rules will largely come down to funding. The CFPB's entire budget for 2014 is roughly 10 percent of the Food and Drug Administration's or 6 percent of the Environmental Protection Agency's. Here is yet another way of thinking about it: the CFPB's budget is equivalent to just 2 percent of what JPMorgan Chase set aside in reserves for its litigation expenses in 2013.

To be sure, the CFPB is making a difference with some of its initiatives. It has, for example, created a "consumer complaint database" where consumers can submit and read complaints about a variety of companies in the financial sector. Banks, creditors, and debt buyers can then use this database to help them decide which collection agencies to hire and not to hire. When it comes to enforcement, however, the CFPB's scope remains somewhat limited because it is focusing almost exclusively on the nation's 175 largest debt collectors. It will thus fall to the state attorneys general to go after many of the smaller operators, which are often the ones acting most egregiously. This is a tall order. Remember that Buffalo—one of the meccas of the industry—is policed by just two full-time employees in the state attorney general's office.

When regulators have acted, they've often concentrated on debt collecting, as opposed to the buying and selling of debt, which is in many regards the real root of the industry's problems. The marketplace for commercial debt remains, in many regards, highly chaotic. Financiers such as Aaron can't rely on the authorities or civil litigation to protect their investors, while debt buyers such as Brandon must make purchases on faith and, when necessary, hunt down the charlatans and threaten them with brute force. Small-time operators such as Jimmy can often buy debt only from dealers like Larry, who don't know—and don't want to know—what it is that they are selling. Debtors like Joanna and Theresa end up paying collectors who don't even own their debts, while others, like Ajay, manage to avoid paying altogether because creditors don't have the proper paperwork.

There is a growing consensus that the marketplace for debt should be made safer, more transparent, and more reliable for both consumers and creditors; the question is, *how?* The most extreme solution is to greatly restrict—or even shut down—the marketplace by barring creditors from reselling their unpaid debts. This seems like a drastic measure and it might not help creditors or consumers. If creditors become less confident that they can minimize their losses by selling off debt they can't collect on themselves, they will inevitably respond by making it more expensive for the least creditworthy consumers (that is, poor people) to borrow money in the first place.

At a roundtable hosted by the FTC and CFPB in 2013, I met two entrepreneurs who were promoting their own solutions. One of them was a former American Express executive named Mark Parsells, who was now the CEO of a company called the Global Debt Registry. The company boasts an easy-to-use central database that tracks the ownership of consumer debts once they are charged off by banks or original creditors. Each debt is assigned a "universal loan identification number," or ULIN, which functions like a "vehicle identification number," or VIN, on a car. When a car changes hands, its license plate number changes, but the VIN remains the same; likewise, when a debt is bought or sold, the account number and the creditor information may change, but the ULIN would remain the same. The registry also maintains electronic records of the original data and documents associated with each debt, such as statements and loan applications. So, when a debt buyer decides to sell a portfolio of debts, it reports the sale—including ULINs for each and every account—to the registry's database. This wouldn't be a public database per se, but if a debtor received an inquiry from a strange collection agency, he or she could access the registry's secure website to verify whether this agency owned the debt or was authorized to collect on it. The registry keeps track of not just credit-card debts but also auto debts, medical debts, and even payday loans. The idea sounded promising, but Parsells told me that it hadn't taken off yet because the big banks and debt buyers were still waiting for more direction from federal regulators.

Many people will be skeptical of trusting a private, profit-driven company to administer the marketplace for consumer debt. And perhaps rightly so. In the world of mortgages, a private company called Mortgage Electronic Registration Systems (or MERS) has attempted to do just this. Lenders embraced MERS because it promised to create such a central registry and, perhaps more enticingly, to save them millions of dollars on paperwork and public recording fees every time a mortgage was bought or sold. The system was fraught with problems, and critics claim that it helped lenders foreclose on many homes improperly. But perhaps this only begs the question: Why can't—or hasn't—the government helped establish such registries? *Isn't it the government's role to minimize chaos, create a safe marketplace, and track the ownership of debt?* After all, the Department of Motor Vehicles tracks who owns what car and the Register of Deeds records who owns a piece of property.

When I visited the FTC in Washington, D.C., I posed this very question to Thomas Kane, an FTC attorney who investigates and brings actions against debt collectors. The question wasn't entirely a fair one, because it was well beyond Kane's purview, but I wondered if *anyone* at the FTC was giving this any thought. "Yeah, I don't know," replied Kane. "The commission hasn't weighed in on something like that. I think that the commission would have to have a lot more information."

Even with stricter government regulation, the industry's savviest actors will find new ways to thrive off debt. This became clear to me one morning, not long ago, when I paid a visit to the legendary Attica prison in upstate New York. I went there to visit an inmate and former debt-collection agency owner named Benny, who remains something of a legend on the East Side of Buffalo. When I mentioned to Jimmy that I was going to meet Benny, even he seemed shocked. "He's a beast," Jimmy told me, with a rare trace of fear in his voice. "He used to be in the BMW boys—big diesel nigger. Wait until you talk to him. He's a goon. What you *going* to talk to him for? That shit cost a nickel."

Upon my arrival at Attica, a guard stamped my hand with invisible ink and told me, "If you don't have that ink on your hand on the way out, you will be spending your nights here until you can prove who you are." A guard then escorted me through a series of huge, clanking, barred gates until I reached the cafeteria, where inmates were allowed to meet with their families.

As I waited for Benny to arrive, I read through his criminal records, which I had obtained from the New York State Department of Corrections. Benny was first incarcerated in 1992 on a first-degree manslaughter charge. During his incarceration, his disciplinary record indicated that he had twenty-eight "misbehavior reports," eleven of which were for drugs. Benny served seventeen years in state prison, got out in 2009, and then was sent back in 2011 on an attempted-robbery charge.

A few minutes later, the guards escorted Benny in. He wore

standard-issue baggy prison pants, which contrasted oddly with his collared, short-sleeved golf shirt. He took a seat and looked out at the cafeteria, where other inmates were now meeting with their wives and their children. "I did seventeen years, so I'm watching guys come in and out," he told me. "They all from my neighborhood, and I watch them come in and out until they can't get back out."

The takeaway from all of this, explained Benny, was that it simply no longer made sense for guys on the street to sell drugs anymore. He added: "I think that there's so much more money on the other side." By the "other side," he meant the lawful side— the world of legitimate business, such as collections. When he was released from prison in 2009, Benny says that he scrounged together $2,500—from friends, family, and savings—and invested it with some guys he knew who had opened up a collection agency. These guys were former criminals who had "changed their lives over."

Collections simply offered a better life, he concluded— much as it had for Brandon, Jimmy, and Larry. During his brief spell of freedom, he claimed that he and his collections industry friends traveled to Miami and "partied out" just "like you see in the rap videos," spending ten thousand dollars on liquor at a single nightclub, enjoying "big hotels, penthouses, big fucking rooms, chicks everywhere on Ocean Drive, you know, the whole South Beach thing." They were living like gangsters, he explained, but they were "legitimate" and could have bank accounts, credit cards, automobiles—all registered in their own names. And this all happened in 2009, he pointed out, when the economy had already tanked.

Benny was reluctant to explain why, just two years later, he went back to jail on an armed-robbery charge. According to his records, he "forcibly stole money at gunpoint inside a residence."

He told me, rather cryptically, that he was only helping a friend. In any case, the money that he had made from his collection agency paid for his criminal defense lawyer. The agency didn't stay up and running for long, however. "They actually shut us down—something happened over there," he told me. Of course, even if a shop got shut down, he explained, the problem wasn't insurmountable. "You know, shut down today and you can get back up tomorrow in another spot somewhere." In comparison with drugs, he explained, the risk was so much lower: "You ain't going to jail—no one's going to jail for that." Even the fines were bearable. "You're making millions of dollars, and they come fine you a hundred twenty thousand dollars—what the fuck is that?"

"Debt's always there," Benny told me with a philosophical air. "You can't get out of debt. Credit is the day's currency. You know what I'm saying? Credit. Without credit you can't get shit." This would never change, he assured me, and there would always be money that needed to be collected from those people who couldn't pay. "Just like hair shops," he explained. "People's hair is going to grow. They always going to want to cut their hair. It's like real estate. People need a place to live. You know what I'm saying?" Americans would continue to live on credit, Benny concluded—the only question was how entrepreneurs like him could create new ways to capitalize on this phenomenon. And Benny had a plan.

"I think the game is evolving," he told me. There was a "transition" occurring, from collections to "refinancing." The future, he told me confidently, belonged to companies that advertised on the radio, Internet, and television, promising to help debtors pay creditors. The beauty of these operations—known as debt-settlement companies—is that the debtors called you, he explained. He then gave me his radio pitch: "*If you got a problem* with your debt, I don't care how many sources it's coming from, give us a call, we'll help you. We can probably get you down to one low loan payment and work out an affordable rate for you." He paused. "This is no different. It's the same shit. It's just a different angle."

I mentioned this idea to Professor Peter Holland, a debt-collections expert at the University of Maryland Law School, to see whether he thought this really was a good "angle." He said that most debt-settlement companies were "total scams." "You basically tell debtors, 'Stop paying all debt and send your money to me and I will work it out for you.'" The catch, says Holland, is that the company often charges exorbitant fees. "I have seen situations where eighty-five percent of the money is going to fees and just fifteen percent is going to escrow," Holland said. The FTC has since banned "up-front fees" like this, he says, but there is still "a lot of room for shady dealings." He concluded that Benny was prescient to target this niche of the collections industry. After all, even if banks stopped selling credit-card accounts to hedge funds and independent collection agencies—and even if the banks cleaned up their practices significantly—debtors would still be looking for "help" paying their bills. "He is ahead of the curve," concluded Holland. "That is where it is going."

Back at Attica, I continued to chat with Benny until—rather suddenly—he seemed to tire of me and said, as if to sum it all up: "In collection, we made pretty good money, man. And that's all I can say. I think we make more money than you would actually [make] selling drugs. It's beautiful."

"And you know"—he paused for a moment and looked at me knowingly—"everything is like a game."

Most of the people whom I met in the course of reporting this book are, in one fashion or another, still in the game. When I last spoke to Jimmy, he had moved his collection agency over to the West Side of Buffalo, so he could distance himself from the crime—and his own past—on the poorer East Side of the city. He was still mainly working payday loans, but he had found a new supplier, who furnished him with good paper—none of which was double-sold. He was also working other people's paper on a contingency basis, keeping 35 percent of what he collected. Profits were up. Even so, he has had problems. Not long ago, he was passing through the East Side, en route to his mother's house, and someone tried to rob him. The incident shook him, in part because he had no real recourse: "I can't act out like I used to—I am a sitting duck out here being legal." This understanding prompted him to purchase a home down in Georgia, where he lives for one week a month, with his girl-friend and their six-month-old son. He passes his days in Georgia barbecuing, gardening, and playing with his baby. "It's peaceful down there," he told me. "So peaceful."

Shafeeq, the Muslim collector whom Aaron hired to help work his paper, ultimately shut down his debt-collection agency and got out of the business altogether. He opted *not* to take a fourth wife and he ended his relationship with his second wife, his former administrative assistant. He now has just two wives, and two separate families with whom he lives on an alternating basis for two days at a time. When I met up with him, at his mosque, he told me that he wanted to invest in "green energy" and that he was spending much of his time praying. "God loves it when you wake up and pray to him. You know what I mean? Because they say he comes out to the lowest level of the heavens and he asks his angels, 'Which one of my servants is up—and what does he want?' And the angel says, 'Oh, this person is.' And he says, 'Give it to him—whatever he wants.' So I just started praying more."

Perhaps not surprisingly, Bill—the agency owner who, somehow or another, managed to get his hands on Aaron's accounts—is still in the business. He shut down the agency where he was working those accounts, but opened a new one in the summer of 2013. When we spoke, later that fall, he lamented the current state of debt collections: "There's no integrity left in this industry, and there was very little to begin with, but now there's none."

A growing problem, said Bill, was that the paper available to small operators like him—mainly payday loans—was increasingly "contaminated." The contamination stemmed from the use by so many collectors of a very aggressive talk-off known as "the shakedown" or "the shake." In this scenario, a collector called up a debtor, introduced himself as a process server, and announced that he was en route to the debtor's house to deliver a summons. The debtor would then, more often than not, become very agitated and ask what this summons was for. The "process server" would then offer a telephone number for the debtor to call and, minutes later, the frantic debtor would be paying his debt. Bill insisted that his agency did not use "the shake," but said that many other agencies in Buffalo did and that this aggressive style of collecting was spreading to Virginia, North Carolina, and Georgia. He mentioned a collector who was banned from New York State and had recently reopened his business in Atlanta. The bottom line for Bill was that it was almost impossible for him to avoid buying contaminated paper—and such paper was worthless. After all, if a debtor didn't pay after the shake, he would never pay.

Eventually, I asked Bill again about the stolen accounts from the Package. "I can still access the whole file if I want," he told me nonchalantly. "I still have it on my database, we're just not collecting [on it]. I don't touch it. It's just been sitting [there] since I don't know when." I asked Bill if he thought it was possible that someone else might have the accounts as well—someone who might resell them. "It could be compromised someway, but I don't think it's been in any of those type of hands," he said. "Like, I'm not a dirty dude, I don't think Brandon is, or anybody else who it really came in contact with. So it should be safe."

Only it wasn't.

In July 2013, debtor #3,159 from the Package—Theresa—received a phone call from a company called McKellar & Associates Group, Inc., trying to collect on the very Washington Mutual debt that she had already paid and that Aaron had definitely retired. The agency was based in Corona, California, and one of its collectors told Theresa that it was collecting the debt on behalf of Chase Bank, which had purchased Washington Mutual in 2008. This was not true. Washington Mutual sold the debt in 2007 and Chase never even owned it. In one call, a collector from McKellar & Associates told Theresa that she was about to be served with legal papers.

It was both galling and astonishing to learn that someone was trying to convince Theresa to pay a debt that she had already paid. In the end, she didn't pay. The question remained: How did her debt end up in their hands? Since Aaron's company had chain of title for her debt—and had retired it—I was totally perplexed as to how McKellar & Associates had any claim to it.

I eventually spoke with Adam Owens, the co-owner of McKellar & Associates. Adam runs a number of different businesses, including his collection agency, which has roughly forty collectors under contract. His main offices are in Beverly Hills. I recounted how one of the agency's collectors had told Theresa that a process server had been hired to deliver legal documents to her door. I asked Adam if this was true. Adam explained that his company did sometimes sue debtors, but not Theresa. He conceded that, if what Theresa said was true, "this was a manipulative tactic the collector used to close the deal." He added, "We have a bonus structure, and you will have people who say things that are not appropriate." This collector, he explained, had since been fired for another matter. Adam added that he always strove for compliance and that his partner had even attended a workshop sponsored by the CFPB.

Eventually, I asked Adam *how* exactly he had obtained Theresa's debt. As it turns out, he had purchased it from a debt broker in Florida. It was part of a much larger package of roughly $50 million worth of debt, which he bought for just twelve basis points—or one-twelfth of a penny on the dollar. It had been bad paper, said Adam, who claims to have gotten burned on the deal. After the purchase, Adam discovered that another agency was collecting on the same paper and, what's more, that some of the charge-off dates had been manipulated so that the debt appeared fresher than it actually was. These problems shouldn't have come entirely as a surprise, however, because he never obtained chain of title for this paper. As Adam saw it, when buying from debt brokers, this was all part of the risk one faced. "It is just data you are purchasing," he told me. "You never know what you are buying." It was rather surreal to see this scenario—similar to the ones I'd seen on the streets of Buffalo—play out in Beverly Hills.

I also checked in with Joanna, the single mom who was raising her daughter in the Midwest. After the incident with Bill and the stolen accounts, Aaron opted to close her account. Perhaps her debt has truly been put to rest, though it might just be a matter of time before she receives a call from an agency like M&A. When I spoke with Joanna, one January evening, she told me that she was still struggling to pay her bills. Her job as a nanny wasn't working out. The money wasn't enough to live on, and to make matters worse, one of her employers' sons had begun to bully her daughter whenever they played together. Joanna needed a new job, but couldn't find one. She told me that the pressure mounted during the holidays: "The night before Christmas Eve, I was off, and we were laying there and watching Christmas movies and making cookies, just trying to have some kind of fun. And [my daughter] was like, 'What's wrong?' And I told her, 'There's a lot going on in our lives, and I'm trying to make it better for us. I'm trying to make sure you have a good life, and it's hard—and sometimes Mommy can't take it anymore.' I was just crying. And you know what she said? She said, 'Let's go for a drive.' So we did. We went for a drive and I showed her where I had applied for a new job, and she was like, 'Okay, I know what it looks like. I'm gonna say a prayer now.'"

Roughly a week later, Joanna got the job, which gave her some cause for optimism. If all went according to plan, she told me, she might be able to pay her utility bill. "My electric I'm hoping to pay next week," she told me. "But maybe not, you know. It might have to wait."

A NOTE ON METHODOLOGY

Perhaps the greatest challenge that I faced in reporting this book was simply getting people to talk to me. Debt collectors are some of the nation's most reviled professionals, and many of them, quite understandably, were reluctant to speak with a journalist and author who might heap more scorn upon their profession. Likewise, many debtors have been so pursued, hounded, and harassed that they were leery of speaking with a stranger who wanted to chronicle, examine, and dissect their financial woes. What's more, some of the people in this book had engaged in activity that was—at the very least—on the edge of legality. For all of these reasons, it was often difficult to encourage subjects to talk about their professional and personal lives with candor.

A few characters were eager to talk from the outset. For them, this book offered a chance to describe the challenges that they faced—professionally, personally, and financially. Aaron Siegel, for instance, was frustrated with his experiences as a debt buyer and was keen to discuss how the system could be improved. Some collectors, like Jimmy, were so tired of being loathed by the public at large that they were desperate to share their stories in the hopes of debunking the stereotype of the debt collector as cold-hearted villain. "If you can show people just how hard my life is and my job is," he told me, "I will be happy."

Whenever possible, I tried to use people's real full names. Many of the characters, including the book's two protagonists—Aaron Siegel and

Brandon Wilson—agreed to this. In other cases, I used first names or nick-names because subjects worried that they might lose business, suffer pro-fessionally, be harassed, or draw unwanted attention from the authorities if they were fully identified. There were several instances where this proved to be impossible, and for these characters (for example, Kenny, Madison, and Lilly), I was forced to use fake names. All of the other details about the people in this book—including their appearances, ages, occupations, personal lives, and places of residence—are entirely true.

There are no composite characters in *Bad Paper*. Each character appear-ing in these pages is a real, singular person whose comments and credibility I assessed carefully before quoting. There is always a danger in quoting people who are not identified or are only partially identified; such partici-pants know that they can speak candidly—which is a good thing—but they also know that if they embellish, or describe another person unfairly, they will likely not be held accountable. When quoting such characters, I was especially careful to corroborate their stories or frame them with an appro-priate degree of skepticism.

In writing this book, I was occasionally required to describe events—from the past—at which I was not present. The most notable example of this is the showdown at Bill's corner store. In this instance, I spoke with virtu-ally everyone who was present at that store. In a situation such as this, there is inevitably a "*Rashomon* effect" as disagreements emerge about the details of what *exactly* transpired. In writing about this event, and others like it, I have tried to attribute quotes specifically and exactly so that it will be clear whose recollection I am relying upon. (For example, in the shouting match between Bill and Brandon, I write: "Bill says that he refused to be strong-armed and that he told Brandon: 'It's not gonna happen here—you're talk-ing to the wrong guy.'") In those instances where I was ultimately unable to discover the truth—for example, how the Package was stolen from Aaron's office—I tried to lay out all of the theories that I deemed credible. In each instance, I have weighed each person's credibility and never assumed that anyone—even one of my main characters—was necessarily telling the truth or recollecting correctly.

Almost all of the financial numbers that I cite relating to what debtors owed and paid are numbers I obtained in paperwork from the banks, or from the courts, or from letters or other communications sent to debtors from creditors. I also consulted the actual Excel spreadsheet connected to the Package. There were just a few exceptions, most notably, the amount of money that Joanna and Theresa claimed to have paid the rogue agency that harassed them. Whenever possible, I have noted where my numbers came from. Both Chase Bank and Bank of America employees, it must be said, were very helpful. The court clerks in Georgia enabled me to track down whatever paperwork existed in each of the cases that I wrote about. In writing this book, I also spoke extensively with federal regulators to ensure that I understood and wrote about their policies as accurately as possible.

NOTES

INTRODUCTION

4 *Some 30 million consumers*: Figures for how much Americans owe come from Federal Reserve Bank of New York, *Quarterly Household Debt and Credit Report*, November 2013. The information about 30 million Americans owing debts, however, comes from remarks made by Richard Cordray, director of the Consumer Financial Protection Bureau, at the Debt Collection Advanced Notice of Proposed Rule Making Press Call on November 6, 2013.

7 *Ever since 2006*: Information on the ranking of consumer complaints by category: The numbers for 2008–2012 come from the FTC's annual *Consumer Sentinel Network Data Book*. The rankings for 2006–2007 can be found in Appendix B2 on page 75 of the 2008 *Consumer Sentinel Network Data Book*.

1. THE $14 MILLION GAMBLE

12 *Buffalo is a major*: Ken Belson, "Collection Agencies Add Scarce Jobs in Hard-Hit Region," *The New York Times*, March 21, 2008.

12 *In the greater Buffalo*: According to the Bureau of Labor Statistics' online database (the Occupational Employment Statistics, or OES), the Buffalo-Niagara Falls area had 5,400 bill and account collectors in 2012. That's more than the number of taxi drivers (600), bakers (500), butchers (320),

steelworkers (320), roofers (560), crane operators (250), hotel clerks (730), and brick masons (170) combined, who total 3,450.

12 *Almost one-third*: New York State Community Action Association, *New York State Poverty Report*, March 2013. "City of Buffalo Poverty Profile . . . Individuals in Poverty: 30.3%."

12 *double the national average*: The U.S. Census Bureau's Official Poverty Measure of 2012 was 15.1 percent, while the Supplemental Poverty Measure, which takes into account government assistance programs for low-income families, was 16 percent (Kathleen Short, "The Research Supplemental Poverty Measure: 2012," U.S. Census Bureau, November 2013).

21 *A 2010 report*: The Legal Aid Society, Neighborhood Economic Development Advocacy Project, MFY Legal Services, and Urban Justice Center, *Debt Deception*, May 2010. "There are as many as 500 privately owned debt buyers in the United States. Little is known about how they finance their operations, though like publicly traded debt buyers, they most likely rely on private investors, commercial loans, and lines of credit."

21 *In financing this purchase*: Lincoln and his business partner William F. Berry actually purchased Radford's store from a man named William Greene, who, earlier that same day, had bought the store from Radford for $400. Greene paid $23 in cash and wrote two promissory notes for $188.50 each. When Lincoln and Berry bought the store from Greene, they paid him $265 in cash, assumed both notes, and also threw in a horse. When the notes matured, Lincoln signed a new promissory note to Radford for $379.82. Radford then assigned this note to Peter Van Bergen, who obtained the judgment against Lincoln. (*Personal Finances of Abraham Lincoln* [The Abraham Lincoln Association, 1943], Harry E. Pratt.) This book can be read online at http://quod.lib.umich.edu/l/lincoln2/5250244.0001.001/1:13?rgn=div1;view=fulltext (see pages 12–13). For information, including dates, I also relied on: *Lincoln's New Salem* (The Abraham Lincoln Association, 1934) by Benjamin P. Thomas; drawings by Romaine Proctor from photographs by the Herbert Georg Studio, Springfield.

22 *One of the early pioneers*: Emily Lambert, "Return of the Billionaire Huckster," *Forbes*, November 2, 2011. "By 1997 CFS owned what Bartmann claims was half the nation's delinquent credit card debt, then worth $15 billion at face value. That year FORBES reckoned Bartmann and his wife were worth $1.1 billion."

22 *He grew up in Dubuque*: Bartmann chronicles his life story in his book, *Bouncing Back: Bill Bartmann, an Autobiography* (Dallas: Brown Books Publishing Group, 2013).

23 *The government seized their assets*: Federal Deposit Insurance Corporation Banking Review, *The Cost of the Savings and Loan Crisis: Truth and Consequences*, December 2000, p. 33. "Over the 1986–1995 period, 1,043 thrifts with total assets of over $500 billion failed." For additional information, see also Lawrence J. White, *The S&L Debacle: Public Policy Lessons for Bank and Thrift Regulation* (Oxford: Oxford University Press, 1992), chapter 2.

24 *"If I set it all on fire"*: Bartmann's boast about how much money he had: Jerry Useem, "The Richest Man You've Never Heard Of," *Inc.*, September 1997; Details about Bartmann's lavish lifestyle during his heyday: Jerry Useem, "How to Lose a Billion," *Fortune*, October 25, 1999.

25 *According to* The New York Times: Information about the demise of CFS: Carol Marie Cropper, "Yes, Even a Bill Collector Can File for Bankruptcy," *The New York Times*, December 20, 1998, Sunday, Late Edition—Final, Section 3, p. 4; Bruce Porter, "A Long Way Down," *The New York Times*, June 6, 2004, Sunday edition, Section 6.

25 *in October, the stock market*: Matt Jarzemsky, "Dow Industrials Set Record," *The Wall Street Journal*, March 5, 2013.

27 *"I'd be a bum"*: Mary Buffett and David Clark, *The Tao of Warren Buffett: Warren Buffett's Words of Wisdom* (Scribner, 2006), p. 121.

3. THE PACKAGE

52 *As of 2010, more than*: Jessica Silver-Greenberg, "Welcome to Debtors' Prison, 2011 Edition," *The Wall Street Journal*, March 17, 2011.

54 *the national average*: The national average of credit cards per consumer was 3.5 in 2008 (Federal Reserve Bank of Boston, *The 2008 Survey of Consumer Payment Choice*, April 2010, p. 9). The national average in 2013 was 2.19 (Experian Information Solutions, *State of Credit: Experian's Fourth Annual Credit Study*, 2013).

57 *Bank of America said*: Jeff Horwitz, "Bank of America Sold Card Debts to Collectors Despite Faulty Records," *American Banker*, March 29, 2012.

58 *An official at Chase Bank*: Information on JPMorgan Chase's acquisition of Washington Mutual: David Enrich, "WaMu Is Seized, Sold Off to J.P. Morgan, in Largest Failure in U.S. Banking History," *The Wall Street Journal*, September 26, 2008.

58 *"When accounts are transferred"*: Federal Trade Commission, "Collecting Consumer Debts: The Challenge of Change," February 2009.

5. AARON'S PROBLEM

73 *According to the National Bureau*: National Bureau of Economic Research, Business Cycle Dating Committee, September 20, 2010. "In determining that a trough occurred in June 2009, the committee did not conclude that economic conditions since that month have been favorable or that the economy has returned to operating at normal capacity. Rather, the committee determined only that the recession ended and a recovery began in that month."

73 *the unemployment rate peaked*: Peter Goodman, "U.S. Unemployment Rate Hits 10.2%, Highest in 26 Years," *The New York Times*, November 6, 2009.

73 *foreclosure notices*: RealtyTrac, "A Record 2.8 Million Receive Foreclosure Notices in 2009," 2009 Year-End Foreclosure Report. (Note: RealtyTrac publishes the monthly U.S. Foreclosure Market Report, which is one of the nation's leading sources of data about foreclosures.)

86 *The Dodd-Frank*: Dodd-Frank Wall Street Reform and Consumer Protection Act of 2010, H.R. 4173, 111th Congress, 2nd Session, 2010. Relevant information can be found in "Title X—Bureau of Consumer Financial Protection."

86 *The idea for the CFPB*: Drake Bennett, "Elizabeth Warren, Champion of Consumer Financial Protection," *Businessweek*, July 7, 2011.

86 *By early 2012, the CFPB*: Consumer Financial Protection Bureau, "CFPB Proposes New Rule to Supervise Larger Participants in Consumer Debt Collection and Consumer Reporting Markets," February 16, 2012.

6. BRANDON'S PEOPLE

89 *Brandon had chosen to*: In Massachusetts, one must apply for a license to run a debt collection business. The state may reject this application if it is "not satisfied [with] the financial responsibility, character, reputation, integrity and general fitness of the applicant." Mass. Gen. Laws ch. 93, § 24b.

105 *The FTC has recommended*: Federal Trade Commission, "Repairing a Broken System," July 2010. See pp. iv and 28.

105 *the vast majority*: There are only a handful of states that require collectors to make some sort of disclosure before they attempt to collect on

an out-of-stat or time-barred debt. And this, of course, remains constantly in flux as states change their laws. As of the writing of this book, in January 2014, states that required disclosures included California, New Mexico, New York, and Massachusetts.

105 *as far as the law is concerned*: The FTC's website says (in its Consumer Information section) this about time-barred or out-of-stat debt: "Although the collector may not sue you to collect the debt, you still owe it. The collector can continue to contact you to try to collect, unless you send a letter to the collector demanding that communication stop." This particular debtor lived in Pennsylvania. The U.S. Court of Appeals for the Third Circuit, which covers Pennsylvania, has ruled that a "debt obligation is not extinguished by the expiration of the statute of limitations, even though the debt is ultimately unenforceable in a court of law." Huertas v. Galaxy Asset Mgmt., 641 F.3d 28 (3d Cir. 2011).

7. SCORING IN VEGAS

116 *mainly payday loans*: Written Testimony of Mike Calhoun (President of Center for Responsible Lending) Before the Senate Banking Committee on "Enhanced Consumer Financial Protection After the Financial Crisis"; Tuesday, July 19, 2011, 538 Dirksen Senate Office Building. The typical "storefront" payday loan has an annual percentage rate of 391 percent.

124 *"purchase and sale agreement"*: Federal Trade Commission vs. Rincon Management Services, LLC. United States District Court, Central District of California, Eastern Division. Case No. ED CV 11—01623 VAP (SPx). This contract was included in the "Supplemental Memorandum of Points and Authorities Re: Receipt of Qualified Overbid for Purchase of the Uncalled Debt Portfolio; Declaration of Richard Weissman in Support Thereof," June 3, 2013.

126 *As of January 2013*: CFPB, "CFPB to Oversee Debt Collectors," October 24, 2012. "The CFPB's supervision authority over these entities will begin when the rule takes effect on January 2, 2013. Under the rule, any firm that has more than $10 million in annual receipts from consumer debt collection activities will be subject to the CFPB's supervisory authority. This authority will extend to about 175 debt collectors, which account for over 60 percent of the industry's annual receipts in the consumer debt collection market."

126 *9,599 debt-collection businesses*: IBISWorld, *Debt Collection Agencies in the US: Market Research Report*, November 2013.

9. THE WHITE MAN'S DOPE

164 *"false threats of lawsuits"*: There were 11,787 complaints in 2008 regarding false threats of lawsuits (Federal Trade Commission, *Federal Trade Commission Annual Report 2009: Fair Debt Collection Practices Act*). There were 30,470 such complaints in 2012 (Consumer Financial Protection Bureau, *Fair Debt Collection Practices Act CFPB Annual Report 2013*, March 20, 2013).

164 *"threats of violence"*: In 2008, there were 1,186 complaints in which "collectors used or threatened to use violence" and 6,404 complaints in which "collectors falsely threatened arrest or seizure of property," for a total of 7,590 complaints in these categories (Federal Trade Commission, *Federal Trade Commission Annual Report 2009: Fair Debt Collection Practices Act*). In 2012, there were 3,312 threats of violence and 24,374 threats of arrest or seizure, for a total of 27,374 complaints (Consumer Financial Protection Bureau, *Fair Debt Collection Practices Act CFPB Annual Report 2013*, March 20, 2013).

165 *a notorious local criminal*: Information on Boyland's arrest and various allegations against him: Robert J. McCarthy, "Raid on a Debt Collector Reaps Not Only Arrest, but Loaded Gun; Cuomo's Office Spearheads Crackdown on Business Tactics," *The Buffalo News*, June 24, 2009; Carolyn Thompson and David B. Caruso, "Buffalo's Debt Collectors Allegedly Using Illegal Tactics to Intimidate Debtors," Associated Press, January 5, 2010.

167 *In 2013, Schneiderman*: Schneiderman made headlines for shutting down an outfit known as International Arbitration Services: Emma Sapong, "State Shuts Down Two Debt Collectors in Buffalo," *The Buffalo News*, February 25, 2013.

10. GEORGIA

184 *If she had to pay 29 percent*: This calculation is based on simple interest, as opposed to compound interest.

190 *The vast majority of deptors*: Three separate studies conducted in New York City indicate that the no-show rate is roughly 90 percent: The Legal Aid Society, Neighborhood Economic Development Advocacy Project, MFY Legal Services, and Urban Justice Center, *Debt Deception: How Debt Buyers Abuse the Legal System to Prey on Lower-Income New Yorkers*, May 2010: "The 26 debt buyers examined in this study

filed 457,322 lawsuits in the New York City Civil Court from January 2006 through July 2008 . . . Debt buyers prevailed in more than nine out of ten lawsuits (94.3%), usually by obtaining default judgments—automatic judgments entered in favor of the debt buyer because the person sued did not appear in court."; MFY Legal Services, Inc., *Justice Disserved: A Preliminary Analysis of the Exceptionally Low Appearance Rate by Defendants in Lawsuits Filed in the Civil Court of the City of New York*, June 2008: "MFY Legal Services, Inc. reviewed available computer data on civil court cases filed in the Bronx, Brooklyn, Queens, and Staten Island in 2007 . . . Of the 180,177 cases filed, only 15,443 (8.57%) defendants appeared in court."; Urban Justice, *Debt Weight: The Consumer Credit Crisis in New York City and Its Impact on the Working Poor*, October 2007: "This study involved a survey of six hundred randomly-selected consumer debt cases filed in February of 2006 in order to increase our understanding of how consumer debt litigation takes place in New York and how it affects New Yorkers . . . Our research found that shockingly few defendants—just 6.7%—in consumer debt cases ever appear in court." In addition, journalists from the *Boston Globe* reported: "About 80 percent of people sued for debts in Massachusetts courts fail to show up at all, according to the estimates of clerks and lawyers and the *Globe*'s observation." The Globe Spotlight Team, "Dignity Faces a Steamroller: Small-Claims Proceedings Ignore Rights, Tilt to Collectors," *Boston Globe*, July 31, 2006.

191 *process servers never*: Ray Rivera, "Suit Claims Fraud by New York Debt Collectors," *The New York Times*, December 30, 2009.

191 *In 2009, the New York*: Jonathon D. Glater, "N.Y. Claims Collectors of Debt Used Fraud," *The New York Times*, July 22, 2009.

192 *In 2013, an FTC study*: FTC, *The Structure and Practices of the Debt Buying Industry*, January 2013, Table 9, p. T-11.

194 *Down in Georgia, creditors*: For debtors, the risk of getting sued over an unpaid debt is quite real. There isn't a great deal of information available about how many consumers are sued each year, but it appears to be a significant number. Encore Capital, one of the nation's largest collection companies, revealed in its 10-K form filed with the SEC that it filed 448,000 lawsuits in 2008—and that was just a single company. This information is available on page 39 of the 10-K filed in 2009.

194 *"meaningfully involved" in the*: Most of the case law involving the "meaningful involvement" standard pertains to collection letters sent

from law firms to debtors. In June 2011, for example, the Third Court of Appeals ruled that settlement letters sent on a law firm's letterhead suggested that a lawsuit was imminent. Such a letter is false or misleading, the court reasoned, unless a lawyer is meaningfully involved in the process. See *Leshner v. The Law Offices of Mitchell N. Fay*, F.3d, 2011 WL 2450964 (3d Cir. 2011). Other courts have also ruled that sending such letters—without meaningful involvement—can be a violation of the section 1692e of the Fair Debt Collection Practices Act. There is, inevitably, debate over what constitutes "meaningful involvement" and how involved a lawyer must be at every step of the collection process.

195 *The state of Georgia*: Norman K. Risjo, *Representative Americans: The Colonists* (Rowman & Littlefield; 2nd ed., May 30, 2001), p. 181; Carol Berkin, Christopher Miller, Robert Cherny, James Gormly, Douglas Egerton, *Making America: A History of the United States* (Cengage Learning; 5th ed., 2013). pp. 71–72.

202 *Over lunch, Shelton*: The information about what Shelton owed Bank of America came directly from the bank. The letter from Sherwin P. Robin & Associates claiming that Shelton owed $8,189 was part of the paperwork filed with the State Court of Richmond County. The judgment for $5,229 is also part of the court's records. The information about Shelton having paid $872 and still owing $6,786 comes from a conversation that Shelton and I had jointly, over the phone, with a representative from Sherwin P. Robin & Associates.

EPILOGUE

212 *"The system for resolving"*: FTC report: The Federal Trade Commission, *Repairing a Broken System: Protecting Consumers in Debt Collection Litigation and Arbitration*, July 2010. Remarks were made by the FTC commissioner, Julie Brill, at an FTC roundtable discussion titled "Life of a Debt: Data Integrity in Debt Collection" on June 6, 2013.

212 *In 2009*: Federal Trade Commission Annual Report 2010: Fair Debt Collection Practices Act, p. 3.

212 *"enforcement action"*: These are the enforcement actions brought by the Federal Trade Commission by year. For 2013: *FTC v. Expert Global Solutions, Inc.*, 3:13-cv-26-2611-M (N.D. Tex. 2013); *FTC v. Security Credit Services, LLC*, 1:13-cv-00799-CC (N.D. Ga. 2013); *FTC v. Goldman Schwartz, Inc.*, 4:13-cv-00106 (S.D. Tex. 2013); *FTC v. Pinnacle Payment*

Services, 1:12-cv-03455-TCB (N.D. Ga. 2013); *FTC v. National Attorney Collections,* 2:13-cv-06212-ODW-VBK (C.D. Calif. 2013); *FTC v. Asset & Capital Management Group,* 8:13-cv-01107-DSF-JC (C.D. Calif. 2013). For 2012: *FTC v. Pro Credit Group, LLC,* 8:12-cv-586-T35-EAJ (M.D. Fla. 2012); *United States v. Luebke Baker & Assocs., Inc.,* Civ. A. 1:12-cv-1145 (C.D. Ill. 2012); *FTC v. Broadway Global Master Inc.,* 2:12-cv-00855-JAM-GGH (E.D. Cal. 2012); *FTC v. AMG Services., Inc.,* 2:12-cv-00536 (D. Nev. 2012); *FTC v. American Credit Crunchers,* 12-cv-1028 (N.D. Ill. 2012); *United States v. Asset Acceptance,* 8:12-cv-182-T-27EAJ (M.D. Fla. 2012). For 2011: *FTC v. Rincon Management Services, LLC,* 5:11-cv-01623-VAP- SP (C.D. Cal. 2011); *FTC v. Forensic Case Management Services, Inc.,* LACV11-7484 RGK (C.D. Cal. 2011); *FTC v. Payday Fin., LLC,* 3:11-cv-3017-RAL (D.S.D. 2011); *United States v. West Asset Mgmt., Inc.,* 1:11-cv-0746 (N.D. Ga. 2011). For 2010: *FTC v. Loan-Pointe, LLC,* 2:10-cv-00225-DAK (D. Utah 2010); *United States v. Credit Bureau Collection Services,* 2:10-cv-169 (S.D. Ohio 2010); *United States v. Allied Interstate, Inc.,* 0:10-cv-04295-PJS-AJB (D. Minn. 2010). For 2009: *United States v. Oxford Collection Agency,* 2:09-cv-02467-LDW-AKT (E.D. N.Y 2009).

213 *The CFPB's budget:* In 2014, the CFPB's estimated budget was $497 million, while the FDA's was $4.7 billion and the EPA's was $8.2 billion.

213 *2 percent:* JPMorgan Chase set aside a $23 billion cushion for litigation reserves in 2013. Peter Lattman and Jessica Silver-Greenberg, "JPMorgan's Loss Is Corporate Law Firms' Gain," *The New York Times,* October 11, 2013.

ACKNOWLEDGMENTS

It was my wife who first encouraged me to write this book. At the time, we were on a train in southern India—with our two small children in tow—and I shared my initial vision for what *Bad Paper* might be. She urged me enthusiastically to press on. I think often of that moment. Without it, this book would not exist. In the days, months, and years since then, she has kindled that spark, helping me believe in my work and make it better.

The other person who was crucial in the early days of this project (and beyond) was my agent, Tina Bennett at WME. If there was a single essential champion for this project—someone who always believed in it and stopped at nothing to make sure that it succeeded—that person was Tina. Superlatives are often flaunted in acknowledgments, but Tina is simply the greatest advocate a writer could have. Also at WME, Svetlana Katz proved time and again to be an excellent reader, advisor, and friend; and Alicia Gordon has been an ideal agent in the realm of television and film rights.

This book began as an article in *The New Yorker*, and here I was aided and encouraged by the legendary Daniel Zalewski. When it came time to find a book publisher, my highest priority was to find an editor who could help me organize the many narratives and ideas in this book and weave them into a single, fluid story. It was a daunting task. Luckily I had the help of Alex Star at FSG, whose commitment to this book was astounding. I still cannot believe how many times he read the manuscript, commented on it, made suggestions, and helped me reshape it. He had an instinct for where I should go with my reporting and my writing, at every step of the way, and his finely tuned inner compass became mine as well. Alex's assistant, Laird Gallagher, was also a great help. I also count myself as very fortunate to be working with my publicist at FSG, Sarita Varma, whose enthusiasm for this book was instant and so greatly appreciated. Lastly, I am thankful to have worked with Samuel Bayard, who provided a keen legal eye.

In writing *Bad Paper*, there were two experts whom I came to rely upon for their keen insights and deep knowledge of the collections industry. The first was Professor Peter Holland at the University of Maryland Law School. On countless occasions, Peter helped me understand how and why the system of debt collection in the United States needed to be changed. He was an inspiration. The second was John H. Bedard, Jr., a Georgia attorney who is one of the smartest and most articulate experts, in any field, that I have ever met. John and I often disagreed on policy and politics, but he influenced my thinking more than he may realize and I am so grateful to have had his help.

This book required a great deal of investigating and I was supported by a number of researchers. They include Chelsea Drake, Asher Hawkins, Summer Austin, Michael Rhoa, Ryan Fagen, Rebecca D. Castagna, Faith Lynn, Kathryn L. Thompson, Jungmoo Lee, and Eric Connelly. I am especially grateful that I had the help of Meagan Flynn, who helped me gather facts, transcribe, fact-check, and edit. Meagan has a gift for editing that belies her youth and which—no doubt—will lead her to do great things.

As I was preparing my manuscript for publication, several friends and family members served as my readers and helped me immeasurably. They include Elaine McArdle, Brian Groh, Tammy Halpern, and Emily Bazelon. These devoted advisors—my mother chief among them—also talked to me constantly on the phone, helping me navigate my way through countless situations. You were truly my colleagues. Thank you. I was also greatly sustained by the support of several other friends, including Peter Kujawinski, Micah Nathan, Aaron Bartley, and Nicholas Dawidoff.

I would also like to thank my family for their support, especially Sebastian Halpern, Lucian Halpern, Tammy Halpern, Paul Zuydhoek, Elizabeth Stanton, Barbara Lipska, Mirek Gorski, Greg Halpern, Ahndraya Parlato, Ava Mae Halpern-Parlato, Witold Lipski, and Cheyenne Noble. I would like to give special thanks to my father, Stephen Halpern, to whom this book is dedicated. His sense of decency has been, and always will be, a guiding light.

Finally, and perhaps most important, this book wouldn't exist if it weren't for all the people who agreed to speak with me, share their stories, their insights, and (often enough) the intimate details of their lives.